Geopolitics: A Very Short Introduction

VERY SHORT INTRODUCTIONS are for anyone wanting a stimulating and accessible way in to a new subject. They are written by experts, and have been published in more than 25 languages worldwide.

The series began in 1995, and now represents a wide variety of topics in history, philosophy, religion, science, and the humanities. Over the next few years it will grow to a library of around 200 volumes – a Very Short Introduction to everything from ancient Egypt and Indian philosophy to conceptual art and cosmology.

Very Short Introductions available now:

AFRICAN HISTORY John Parker and Richard Rathbone
AMERICAN POLITICAL PARTIES AND ELECTIONS L. Sandy Maisel
THE AMERICAN PRESIDENCY Charles O. Jones
ANARCHISM Colin Ward
ANCIENT EGYPT Ian Shaw
ANCIENT PHILOSOPHY Julia Annas
ANCIENT WARFARE Harry Sidebottom
ANGLICANISM Mark Chapman
THE ANGLO-SAXON AGE John Blair
ANIMAL RIGHTS David DeGrazia
ARCHAEOLOGY Paul Bahn
ARCHITECTURE Andrew Ballantyne
ARISTOTLE Jonathan Barnes
ART HISTORY Dana Arnold
ART THEORY Cynthia Freeland
THE HISTORY OF ASTRONOMY Michael Hoskin
ATHEISM Julian Baggini
AUGUSTINE Henry Chadwick
BARTHES Jonathan Culler
BESTSELLERS John Sutherland
THE BIBLE John Riches
THE BRAIN Michael O'Shea
BRITISH POLITICS Anthony Wright
BUDDHA Michael Carrithers
BUDDHISM Damien Keown
BUDDHIST ETHICS Damien Keown
CAPITALISM James Fulcher
THE CELTS Barry Cunliffe
CHAOS Leonard Smith
CHOICE THEORY Michael Allingham
CHRISTIAN ART Beth Williamson
CHRISTIANITY Linda Woodhead
CLASSICS Mary Beard and John Henderson

CLASSICAL MYTHOLOGY
Helen Morales
CLAUSEWITZ Michael Howard
THE COLD WAR
Robert McMahon
CONSCIOUSNESS
Susan Blackmore
CONTEMPORARY ART
Julian Stallabrass
CONTINENTAL PHILOSOPHY
Simon Critchley
COSMOLOGY Peter Coles
THE CRUSADES
Christopher Tyerman
CRYPTOGRAPHY
Fred Piper and Sean Murphy
DADA AND SURREALISM
David Hopkins
DARWIN Jonathan Howard
THE DEAD SEA SCROLLS
Timothy Lim
DEMOCRACY Bernard Crick
DESCARTES Tom Sorell
DESIGN John Heskett
DINOSAURS David Norman
DOCUMENTARY FILM
Patricia Aufderheide
DREAMING J. Allan Hobson
DRUGS Leslie Iversen
THE EARTH Martin Redfern
ECONOMICS Partha Dasgupta
EGYPTIAN MYTH
Geraldine Pinch
EIGHTEENTH-CENTURY BRITAIN Paul Langford
THE ELEMENTS Philip Ball
EMOTION Dylan Evans
EMPIRE Stephen Howe
ENGELS Terrell Carver
ETHICS Simon Blackburn
THE EUROPEAN UNION
John Pinder
EVOLUTION
Brian and Deborah Charlesworth
EXISTENTIALISM
Thomas Flynn
FASCISM Kevin Passmore
FEMINISM Margaret Walters
THE FIRST WORLD WAR
Michael Howard
FOSSILS Keith Thomson
FOUCAULT Gary Gutting
THE FRENCH REVOLUTION
William Doyle
FREE WILL Thomas Pink
FREUD Anthony Storr
FUNDAMENTALISM
Malise Ruthven
GALILEO Stillman Drake
GANDHI Bhikhu Parekh
GEOPOLITICS Klaus Dodds
GLOBAL CATASTROPHES
Bill McGuire
GLOBALIZATION
Manfred Steger
GLOBAL WARMING
Mark Maslin
THE GREAT DEPRESSION AND THE NEW DEAL
Eric Rauchway

HABERMAS James Gordon Finlayson
HEGEL Peter Singer
HEIDEGGER Michael Inwood
HIEROGLYPHS Penelope Wilson
HINDUISM Kim Knott
HISTORY John H. Arnold
HOBBES Richard Tuck
HUMAN EVOLUTION Bernard Wood
HUMAN RIGHTS Andrew Clapham
HUME A. J. Ayer
IDEOLOGY Michael Freeden
INDIAN PHILOSOPHY Sue Hamilton
INTELLIGENCE Ian J. Deary
INTERNATIONAL MIGRATION Khalid Koser
INTERNATIONAL RELATIONS Paul Wilkinson
ISLAM Malise Ruthven
JOURNALISM Ian Hargreaves
JUDAISM Norman Solomon
JUNG Anthony Stevens
KABBALAH Joseph Dan
KAFKA Ritchie Robertson
KANT Roger Scruton
KIERKEGAARD Patrick Gardiner
THE KORAN Michael Cook
LINGUISTICS Peter Matthews
LITERARY THEORY Jonathan Culler
LOCKE John Dunn
LOGIC Graham Priest
MACHIAVELLI Quentin Skinner
THE MARQUIS DE SADE John Phillips
MARX Peter Singer
MATHEMATICS Timothy Gowers
MEDICAL ETHICS Tony Hope
MEDIEVAL BRITAIN John Gillingham and Ralph A. Griffiths
MODERN ART David Cottington
MODERN IRELAND Senia Pašeta
MOLECULES Philip Ball
MUSIC Nicholas Cook
MYTH Robert A. Segal
NATIONALISM Steven Grosby
THE NEW TESTAMENT AS LITERATURE Kyle Keefer
NEWTON Robert Iliffe
NIETZSCHE Michael Tanner
NINETEENTH-CENTURY BRITAIN Christopher Harvie and H. C. G. Matthew
NORTHERN IRELAND Marc Mulholland
PARTICLE PHYSICS Frank Close
PAUL E. P. Sanders
PHILOSOPHY Edward Craig
PHILOSOPHY OF LAW Raymond Wacks
PHILOSOPHY OF SCIENCE Samir Okasha
PHOTOGRAPHY Steve Edwards
PLATO Julia Annas

POLITICS Kenneth Minogue
POLITICAL PHILOSOPHY David Miller
POSTCOLONIALISM Robert Young
POSTMODERNISM Christopher Butler
POSTSTRUCTURALISM Catherine Belsey
PREHISTORY Chris Gosden
PRESOCRATIC PHILOSOPHY Catherine Osborne
PSYCHOLOGY Gillian Butler and Freda McManus
PSYCHIATRY Tom Burns
QUANTUM THEORY John Polkinghorne
RACISM Ali Rattansi
THE RENAISSANCE Jerry Brotton
RENAISSANCE ART Geraldine A. Johnson
ROMAN BRITAIN Peter Salway
THE ROMAN EMPIRE Christopher Kelly
ROUSSEAU Robert Wokler
RUSSELL A. C. Grayling
RUSSIAN LITERATURE Catriona Kelly
THE RUSSIAN REVOLUTION S. A. Smith
SCHIZOPHRENIA Chris Frith and Eve Johnstone
SCHOPENHAUER Christopher Janaway
SHAKESPEARE Germaine Greer
SIKHISM Eleanor Nesbitt
SOCIAL AND CULTURAL ANTHROPOLOGY John Monaghan and Peter Just
SOCIALISM Michael Newman
SOCIOLOGY Steve Bruce
SOCRATES C. C. W. Taylor
THE SPANISH CIVIL WAR Helen Graham
SPINOZA Roger Scruton
STUART BRITAIN John Morrill
TERRORISM Charles Townshend
THEOLOGY David F. Ford
THE HISTORY OF TIME Leofranc Holford-Strevens
TRAGEDY Adrian Poole
THE TUDORS John Guy
TWENTIETH-CENTURY BRITAIN Kenneth O. Morgan
THE VIKINGS Julian Richards
WITTGENSTEIN A. C. Grayling
WORLD MUSIC Philip Bohlman
THE WORLD TRADE ORGANIZATION Amrita Narlikar

Available soon:

ANTISEMITISM Steven Beller
THE EUROPEAN UNION (NEW EDITION) John Pinder and Simon Usherwood
EXPRESSIONISM Katerina Reed-Tsocha
GALAXIES John Gribbin
GAME THEORY Ken Binmore
GEOGRAPHY John Matthews and David Herbert
GERMAN LITERATURE Nicholas Boyle
HIV/AIDS Alan Whiteside
THE MEANING OF LIFE Terry Eagleton
MEMORY Jonathan Foster
MODERN CHINA Rana Mitter
NUCLEAR WEAPONS Joseph M. Siracusa
QUAKERISM Pink Dandelion
SCIENCE AND RELIGION Thomas Dixon
SEXUALITY Véronique Mottier

For more information visit our web site

www.oup.co.uk/general/vsi/

Klaus Dodds

GEOPOLITICS

A Very Short Introduction

OXFORD
UNIVERSITY PRESS

Great Clarendon Street, Oxford OX2 6DP

Oxford University Press is a department of the University of Oxford.
It furthers the University's objective of excellence in research, scholarship,
and education by publishing worldwide in

Oxford New York

Auckland Cape Town Dar es Salaam Hong Kong Karachi
Kuala Lumpur Madrid Melbourne Mexico City Nairobi
New Delhi Shanghai Taipei Toronto

With offices in

Argentina Austria Brazil Chile Czech Republic France Greece
Guatemala Hungary Italy Japan Poland Portugal Singapore
South Korea Switzerland Thailand Turkey Ukraine Vietnam

Published in the United States
by Oxford University Press Inc., New York

First Published as a Very Short Introduction 2007

British Library Cataloguing in Publication Data
Data available

Library of Congress Cataloging in Publication Data
Data available

ISBN 978–0–19–920658–2

10 9 8 7 6 5 4 3 2 1

Typeset by SPI Publisher Services, Pondicherry, India
Printed in Great Britain
on acid-free paper by
Ashford Colour Press Ltd, Gosport, Hampshire

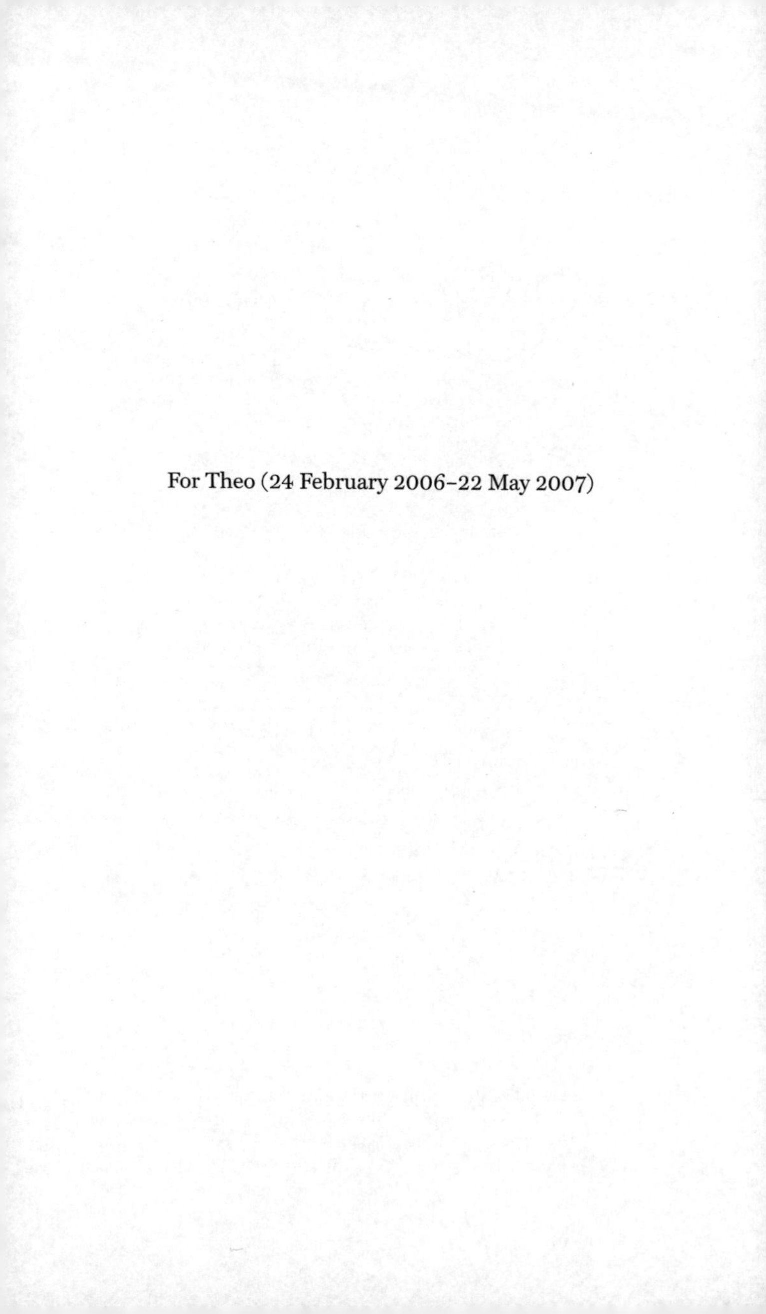

For Theo (24 February 2006–22 May 2007)

Acknowledgements

I am indebted to many people who, in their different ways, have assisted me in the writing of this book. My colleagues at Royal Holloway, University of London have helped provide a congenial academic home for over 12 years and I thank in particular Philip Beesley and Felix Driver. I am also indebted to my geopolitical and historical colleagues including Luiza Bialasiewicz, Jason Dittmer, Fraser MacDonald, Mike Heffernan, and Francis Robinson CBE for their supportive comments. In particular, I want to acknowledge my former doctoral supervisor and mentor, the late Professor Leslie Hepple (1947–2007). Thanks also to the Oxford University Press team including Luciana O'Flaherty, Jane Robson, James Thompson and Helen Oakes for their support and enthusiasm.

The Leverhulme Trust through the award of the Philip Leverhulme Prize enabled me to enjoy extended research leave (2006–8). I am most grateful for their support.

On a more personal note, my mother provided many insights and words of support. My wife Carolyn continues to be wonderfully understanding of a wandering academic obsessed with all things geopolitical. Our neighbours Tina, Claire, Nicola, and Dan provided much support during the difficult process of writing this book.

Finally, I would like to thank the marvellous consultants, doctors, and nursing staff associated with the paediatric intensive care unit at the Royal Brompton Hospital for their dedicated care of our youngest son, Theo. Thanks to their dedication and professionalism, he recovered from major heart surgery in November 2006 and I was able to complete this book as a consequence. Tragically, Theo later died in May 2007. During his last few days, he received dedicated care from the doctors and nursing staff attached to the paediatric intensive care unit at the Evelina Children's Hospital.

This book is dedicated to our wonderful son Theo for bringing us so much joy. It was an honour and privilege being his father.

Contents

List of illustrations

The publisher and the author apologize for any errors or omissions in the above list. If contacted they will be pleased to rectify these at the earliest opportunity.

Chapter 1
It's smart to be geopolitical!

While the title of this opening chapter may appear to be a little self-serving and owes its origins to Robert Strausz-Hupe, the founder of the right-wing Foreign Policy Research Institute in the United States, I aim to convince you that it is not only smart but also essential to be geopolitical. Amid the ongoing bloodshed in Afghanistan, Iraq, Sudan, and less well reported places such as the Congo, the continued relevance of geopolitics is overwhelming. Despite the claims made in favour of ever more intense forms of globalization, the relevance of territory, international boundaries, and claims to sovereignty remain as pressing as ever. A few feet here or there can mean the matter of life and/or death. The labelling of a particular place as 'dangerous' and/or 'threatening' can invite military assaults from land, sea, and air, as civilians found to their cost in southern Lebanon in the summer of 2006. Even America's allies in the midst of a Global War on Terror such as Pakistan, according to President Pervez Musharraf, have occasionally faced the unpleasant prospect of being 'bombed back to the stone age' if their commitment to root out terrorists and their networks ever wavered.

For those of us living in Europe and North America, geopolitics might at first appear to have less relevance – something to be applied to more turbulent areas of the world. This is a mistaken view. Geopolitics is also part of our everyday lives and by 'our' I

1. Beirut suburbs slowly come back to life after weeks of bombing in 2006

mean those readers who might be better able to insulate themselves to the sometimes daily struggles to cross borders, assert ownership over land, and prevent flows of unwanted armed personnel and/or suicide bombers. While some British and North American citizens might worry at the new biometric security checks at airports and seaports, the impact of the 11 September 2001 attacks on the United States was wide reaching. The subsequent suicide bomb attacks in Bali, Casablanca, Istanbul, Jerusalem, London, and Madrid, in combination with the deeply controversial Anglo-American invasion of Iraq, have highlighted how places and people are interconnected with one another. Cities in particular have borne the brunt of this collective assault and none more than Iraqi cities such as Baghdad, Fallujah, and Mosul whose citizens endure near daily assaults by suicide bombers, death squads, and coalition forces. Since March 2003, over 650,000 Iraqis have been killed, 2 million displaced and 10 million remain without access to clean water, according to some estimates by non-governmental organizations.

Every week, I receive leaflets in the mail, urging me to support vulnerable communities such as those in southern Lebanon, Iraq, Palestine, or Afghanistan. Some places can, quite literally, be demanding of our attention, while others such as Mogadishu (the capital of Somalia) are more likely to be encountered electronically – watch the movie, *Black Hawk Down* (2001) and now play the video game. If we are entering a new age of 'blood and iron' then it is important that we better understand those real and virtual connections between places and communities and the consequences that follow therein. Geopolitics, precisely because it is preoccupied with borders, resources, flows, territories, and identities, can provide a pathway for critical analysis and understanding – albeit a controversial one.

But what exactly is geopolitics? If you were to Google the term 'geopolitics' at any one time, you might receive approximately six to seven million hits. Anyone brave or perhaps foolish enough to wade through even a fraction of those potential references would not necessarily emerge any the wiser with regards to a definition of geopolitics. To paraphrase the social theorist Michael Mann, geopolitics, like most terms that have attracted academic attention, is slippery. More often than not, it is used by journalists and pundits such as Thomas Barnett of the *Esquire* magazine, Thomas Friedman of the *New York Times,* or the former US Secretary of State Henry Kissinger as a shorthand term, intended to convey a robust attitude towards political action using taken-for-granted geographical templates such as the 'axis of evil' and 'outposts of tyranny'. Rather than take those terms for granted (or simply mock them), it is vital that we explore the sorts of consequences that follow from dividing the world into particular zones.

Towards an understanding of geopolitics

Geopolitics provides ways of looking at the world and is highly visual as a consequence, readily embracing maps, tables, and photographs. While there is really little point in trying to establish a definition of the term that would be able to hold a consensus of opinion amongst pundits, two distinct understandings of geopolitics will suffice for the purpose of this very short introduction. First, geopolitics offers for many a reliable guide of the global landscape using geographical descriptions, metaphors, and templates such as 'iron curtain', 'Third World', and/or 'rogue state'. Each of these terms is inherently geographical because places are identified and labelled as such. It then helps to generate a simple model of the world, which can then be used to advise and inform foreign and security policy making. This idea of geopolitics is by far the most important in terms of everyday usage in newspapers, radio, magazines, and television news, which also tends to reduce governments and countries to simple descriptors such as 'London', 'Washington', or 'Moscow'.

Second, we could focus our attention on how geopolitics actually works as an academic and popular practice. So rather than simply assume that labels such as 'iron curtain' and 'axis of evil' have a certain heuristic value, we proceed to question how they generate particular understandings of places, communities, and accompanying identities. The term 'Third World', for example, not only served as a geographical description of many places in Africa, Asia, and Latin America, it also helped to triangulate the political geographies of the cold war involving the United States and the 'First World' and the Soviet Union and the 'Second World' in a global competition. While some have criticized the term for assuming that the 'Third World' was the open space for further expressions of superpower rivalry, others including leaders and intellectuals located in Africa, Asia, and Latin America embraced the term as a means of registering their political and geographical difference from the Global North.

This book inherently favours the second approach over the first and thus does not seek to provide a geopolitical guide to Western foreign policy making. It makes no pretence to being allied to the ongoing endeavours of the Cambridge-based Henry Jackson Society, which has recently proposed a new form of 'democratic geopolitics' for British foreign policy. While they have used the term geopolitics, they show no interest in exploring the nature of the term. Rather, the aim here is to show how geopolitics gets used and with what consequences especially in everyday life. In the main, geopolitical writers take the global stage as their starting point. The appeal of a 'god's eye view of world' can often prove irresistible to leaders and pundits of all political persuasions and backgrounds. At times of global crises and war, it is understandable that such a global view of the world might need to prevail. Consider, for instance, some of the speeches made by Prime Minister Winston Churchill and President Harry Truman in the mid to late 1940s. Political and geographical context was critical as both sought to interpret a world that had been ravaged by conflict. Allied victory had not brought global stability. Within three years of the ending of the Second World War, the victorious powers were embroiled in a crisis over access to the divided city of Berlin. By the time five years had elapsed, those same wartime allies alongside China were confronting one another in the Korean Peninsula. Over two million people died as a consequence and most of the victims were civilian. The Peninsula remains divided to this day along the 38th Parallel.

In March 1946, before the crises in Berlin and Korea, Churchill addressed an audience in Fulton in the state of Missouri. Taking stock of the world, and Europe in particular, Churchill evoked (but did not coin) one of the most memorable expressions of the 20th century:

> From Stettin in the Baltic to Trieste in the Adriatic *an iron curtain* has descended across the Continent. Behind that line lie all the capitals of the ancient states of Central and Eastern Europe. Warsaw, Berlin, Prague, Vienna, Budapest, Belgrade, Bucharest and Sofia; all these famous cities and the populations around them lie in what I must call the Soviet sphere, and all are subject, in one form or another, not only to Soviet influence but to a very high and in some cases increasing measure of control from Moscow.
>
> Twice the United States has had to send several millions of its young men across the Atlantic to fight the wars. But now we all can find any nation, wherever it may dwell, between dusk and dawn. Surely we should work with conscious purpose for a grand pacification of Europe within the structure of the United Nations and in accordance with our Charter.

The term 'iron curtain' attracted much public attention in the immediate aftermath. As an analogy, the phrase conveyed a very real sense of a geographical barrier cutting across a vast swathe of continental Europe. Critically, a curtain made of iron not only prevents light from filtering through it but also foils any other flows such as people and/or goods. Churchill often made reference to light and darkness in his wartime and cold war speeches in order to convey a further sense of how Europe was divided between liberal democracies in the West and fascism and later communist regimes in the East. The 'iron curtain' stuck in the geographical imaginations of people both sides of the Atlantic and was later to be supplemented by President Reagan's description of the Soviet Union as an 'evil empire' in 1982. By way of contrast, the Soviet media never published Churchill's speech and the Soviet leader Joseph Stalin later used 'the speech' to persuade his fellow citizens that the country was being threatened by an aggressive grouping comprised of the United States and its Western European allies including Britain.

President Truman, a contemporary of Churchill and Stalin, also used his speeches to represent and interpret a world that was changing in the late 1940s. In an address on 12 March 1947 to a joint session of Congress, Truman presented a stark view of the world:

> At the present moment in world history nearly every nation must choose between alternative *ways of life*. The choice is too often not a free one.
>
> One way of life is based upon the will of the majority, and is distinguished by free institutions, representative government, free elections, [and] guarantees of individual liberty, freedom of speech and religion, and freedom from political oppression.
>
> The second way of life is based upon the will of a minority forcibly imposed upon the majority. It relies upon terror and oppression, a controlled press and radio; fixed elections, and the suppression of personal freedoms.
>
> I believe that it must be the policy of the United States to support free peoples who are resisting attempted subjugation by armed minorities or by outside pressures.

> I believe that we must assist free peoples to work out their own destinies in their own way.
>
> I believe that our help should be primarily through economic and financial aid, which is essential to economic stability and orderly political processes.
>
> The world is not static, and the status quo is not sacred. But we cannot allow changes in the status quo in violation of the Charter of the United Nations by such methods as coercion, or by such subterfuges as political infiltration. In helping free and independent nations to maintain their freedom, the United States will be giving effect to the principles of the Charter of the United Nations. It is necessary only to glance at a map to realize that the survival and integrity of the Greek nation are of grave importance in a much wider situation. If Greece should fall under the control of an armed minority, the effect upon its neighbor, Turkey, would be immediate and serious. Confusion and disorder might well spread throughout the entire Middle East.

As with Churchill's address, the speech was instrumental in shaping the post-1945 geographical imagination of the United States and the wider world. After examining the fragile situation in Greece and Turkey, the President offered a simple but politically effective division ('ways of life') between those countries that supported liberty, freedom, and democracy and those who did not. While it was clear that he intended the division to favour the United States and its allies at the expense of the Soviet Union, it also committed the country to upholding the new geopolitical architecture of the post-1945 era. American support in the 1940s and 1950s was critical even if more contemporary administrations have been prone to displays of ambivalence and even thinly disguised malfeasance towards the United Nations.

Terms such as 'iron curtain' and later geographical manifestations such as 'evil empire' under President Reagan in the 1980s or 'axis of evil' under President George W. Bush in 2002 matter greatly because they frequently help to legitimate (and justify) subsequent expressions of statesmanship and foreign policy decision making. Geographical descriptions continue to provide an essential element in the implementation of foreign and security policies. Those descriptions of places and regions can also be dramatically overturned by events. The destruction of the Berlin Wall in November 1989 led to a radical re-evaluation of Eastern and Central Europe by American and Russian governments alike. The term 'iron curtain' no longer made political and/or geographical sense as democratic movements brushed former communist regimes aside. Two years later, the so-called 'evil empire' of the Soviet Union disintegrated and the cold war security organization, the North Atlantic Treaty Organization (NATO, created in 1949), expanded to include former Eastern Bloc states such as Poland, Czech Republic, and Hungary. The Russian government has looked on with mounting concern at this geopolitical encroachment.

Geopolitics, as I noted earlier, can also concern itself with the implicit geographical understandings of world politics mobilized every day by political leaders, journalists, and learned experts. Terms such as 'Third World' not only served to identify particular regions of the world but also aided and abetted the production and circulation of cold war identities. Recently independent countries in Africa and Asia used expressions such as 'non-alignment' to depict a desire for different sets of geographical and ideological relationships – ones which were not tied to the two superpowers. While it may be perfectly reasonable to focus on the speeches and subsequent behaviour of powerful political leaders, geopolitical activities are not the sole preserve of states and governments. Individuals, non-governmental organizations, private companies, international and regional institutions such as the United Nations and the European Union engage in geopolitics. New media technologies such as the internet have also enabled non-state organizations, such as anti-globalization groups and terror networks amongst others, to use it to campaign and mobilize public support for different political geographical representations of the world.

This notion of geographical imagination is significant and owes much to the writings of the late Palestinian-American scholar, Edward Said. In his many works including *Orientalism* (1978), Said articulated an interest in how places were and continue to be imagined and represented in art, literature, music, and western foreign policy making. As a committed advocate of a Palestinian state, he was deeply sensitive to how communities such as the Palestinians or the wider Arabic world were understood, often in unflattering terms, as unstable, threatening, and/or exotic. This meant, he suggested, that particular cultural understandings of place and communities, could rally policy makers and public opinion in ways that might be antithetical to the project of achieving an autonomous Palestinian community. Writing for much of his life in the United States, Said was deeply concerned that the mainstream media in that country was unsympathetic to the plight of the Palestinians and more likely to regard them as harbourers of terrorists than part of a dispossessed people confined to refugee camps or, like himself, part of a wider diaspora. If Palestinians are understood in unflattering terms then it becomes all the easier for others such as pro-Israeli supporters to marginalize attempts to draw attention to the continued occupation of the West Bank or the consequences of the Israeli-built security wall. Who would wish to support a people labelled as harbourers of terrorists?

Video games and virtual Afghanistan and Iraq

Interested readers might like to consult the following website (www.kumawar.org) and see the range of video games on offer to participants eager to recreate American military engagements in Iraq and Afghanistan, including the assault on Fallujah in 2004. Users are encouraged to use satellite

imagery and mapping so that they can plan their own military campaigns, and the company responsible for product development encourages real-life soldiers to volunteer their stories about combat experiences. Iraqi civilians and/or suspected militants appear to be either obstacles and/or adversaries that need to be killed, usually in large numbers.

Geographical representations help to inform people's understandings of the world and in that sense we are all geopolitical theorists. Critically, however, our geographical understandings of the world may differ radically and for a host of reasons – religious, ethnic, political, and so on. Muslims might remind us that one of the most important elements of their collective geographical imaginations is the notion of the umma, a community of fellow believers that stretches across North Africa, Europe, and Asia in particular. Some Muslims might also have pictures of Mecca and Medina in their living rooms. International bodies such as the Organization of the Islamic Conference (OIC), created in 1969 (or 1390 according to the Muslim calendar), exist specifically to provide a forum for an alternative response to a world that is usually defined by powerful Christian countries such as the United States and their visions of global order. Incidentally, if you were to access the home page of the OIC, you will notice that the motif of the OIC is juxtaposed on the global symbol of the United Nations (www.oic-oic.org).

Linking geopolitics to popular culture

Geopolitics is neither something that simply occurs in the State Department nor that which is reproduced in the opinion pieces of newspapers such as the *New York Times* and the *Guardian*. Take the State of the Union address as an example. The American President always gives this address to a Joint Session of the House of Congress in January of each year. It is a high-profile opportunity for a President to convey his vision for the country and the wider world. As part of that *tour d'horizon*, the State of the Union address frequently utilizes a whole series of geopolitical codes in order to rank countries and regions in order of their geographical significance, ranging from major allies to those considered to be clear and present dangers. The speech is televised and subject to extensive analysis in newspapers and magazines. Moreover, coming from the leader of the most powerful state in the world, presidential speeches also enjoy extensive contemplation from international media organizations. As such, the State of the Union address becomes part of everyday life and hence the subject of conversations in the home, the office, and the café.

Speaking in January 2002, only a few months after the 11 September attacks on the United States, the President's State of the Union address was a momentous event as many citizens looked to their Commander-in-Chief to make sense of events. American citizens were still in a state of shock. How was the President going to both reassure the populace and reassert America's sense of self-importance? As the speech unfolded, Bush deployed the following explicit geopolitical evaluation:

> Our second goal is to prevent regimes that sponsor terror from threatening America or our friends and allies with weapons of mass destruction. Some of these regimes have been pretty quiet since September the 11th. But we know their true nature. North Korea is a regime arming with missiles and weapons of mass destruction, while starving its citizens.
>
> Iran aggressively pursues these weapons and exports terror, while an unelected few repress the Iranian people's hope for freedom.
>
> Iraq continues to flaunt its hostility toward America and to support terror. The Iraqi regime has plotted to develop anthrax, and nerve gas, and nuclear weapons for over a decade. This is a regime that has already used poison gas to murder thousands of its own citizens – leaving the bodies of mothers huddled over their dead

children. This is a regime that agreed to international inspections – then kicked out the inspectors. This is a regime that has something to hide from the civilized world.

> ... I will not stand by, as peril draws closer and closer. The United States of America will not permit the world's most dangerous regimes to threaten us with the world's most destructive weapons. (Applause)

This section of the address caused much interest amongst media and political commentators not least because of the phrase 'axis of evil' to describe the trio of Iran, Iraq, and North Korea. When the President of the United States and Commander-in-Chief of the US Armed Forces describes three countries as part of an 'axis of evil', people all over the world tend to notice. Unsurprisingly, the governments of those three countries strongly criticized the address and denounced the United States in public addresses designed in the main to reassure domestic audiences. From the President's point of view, the phrase 'axis of evil' was not only intended to act as a proverbial 'shot across the bows' of states that the United States disapproved of but also provided a simple geographical template of the world. By the time the President returned to this theme in the 2003 State of the Union address, Saddam Hussein in particular had been identified as a 'brutal dictator, with a history of reckless aggression ... with ties to terrorism ... [he] will not be permitted to dominate a vital region and threaten the United States'.

While few would seriously contend that Saddam Hussein was not brutal, this description, alongside many others, was important in preparing the 'ground' for the invasion in March 2003. The link to terrorism and weapons of mass destruction proved enticing to many Americans, who initially supported President Bush's decision to take military action. While many experts in North America and elsewhere were doubtful of such connections, public opinion was not sufficiently critical of those assertions to prevent the sceptics within the United States from overturning this element of the Global War on Terror. Why? In part it may well be that many Americans were simply not willing to call into question the judgement of the President and his colleagues such as Dick Cheney. To do so, one might have been labelled 'unpatriotic' and, with a reminder from the days of the cold war, 'un-American' – a charge levelled at musicians, actors, and intellectuals such as the Dixie Chicks, Martin Sheen, and Noam Chomsky respectively.

A factor that might also have had some relevance was the mainstream print and television media, which overwhelmingly supported the Bush administration. A large proportion of Americans rely on television for their news and most of those viewers are neither well travelled nor do they access alternative media sources such as online newspapers in other parts of the English-speaking world. It is sometimes difficult for non-American observers to believe that over 80 per cent of American citizens do not possess a passport, as many European and other global cities seem to have their fill of US visitors. As a consequence, American presidents have often used simple geographical descriptions and terms to convey a sense of geopolitical difference between their country and others, such as contemporary Iran or the Soviet Union in the recent past.

The 2002 State of the Union address mattered greatly because it helped to cement in the minds of many that the regime of Saddam Hussein in Iraq was connected to the 11 September 2001 attacks. Despite there being no clear evidence to link that regime to Islamic militancy and terror networks, many Americans were content to accept the geographical linkage and this in turn helped the administration to persuade their citizens that an invasion of Iraq, after the earlier military action in Afghanistan, was a vital next step in winning the Global War on Terror. While it is perfectly clear that not all Americans were duped into accepting this vision of the world, as the broadcasts aired on National Public Radio and Public Broadcasting Service would testify, sufficient numbers were

2. President George W. Bush on the USS *Abraham Lincoln*, 1 May 2003

prepared to accept the words and behaviour of their President and Commander-in-Chief.

In November 2004, much to the disappointment of many American voters, presidential candidate John Kerry was not able to deny the George W. Bush administration a second term. Sufficient numbers of voters were persuaded that the Republican Party was better able to secure America from the threat of terrorism. Perhaps popular culture did not help the Democrats in the sense that some of the biggest Hollywood hits such as *Die Another Day* (2002), *Collateral Damage* (2002), and *Sum of All Fears* (2001) depicted the United States as gravely imperilled by a host of terrorists and governments scattered across the globe, including North Korea and the Middle East. Even the British super-spy, James Bond, was working with his American colleagues to prevent a crazed North Korean colonel from eradicating South Korea and Japan with a powerful and destructive satellite. In the aftermath of the release of *Die Another Day* (2002), representatives of the North Korean regime remonstrated with the

3. James Bond and *Die Another Day* (2002)

United States because of the film's depiction of North Korean personnel threatening to destroy large parts of East Asia. The film coincided with the American President's description of their country as part of an 'axis of evil'. Combined with the ongoing efforts of the Department of Homeland Security and its security briefings and colour-coded representations of threat, many Americans were unwilling to change the presidential leadership in the midst of great uncertainty – real and/or perceived.

American presidents are not unique in terms of using simple geographical templates. When President Ahmadinejad of Iran told 4,000 student listeners in October 2005 that Israel must be 'wiped off the map', he was not just talking to them about the geopolitical ambitions of Iran. His public denunciation of Israel and his oft-stated desire to rewrite the political map of the Middle East provoked an angry reaction in Israel and its allies such as the United States. For international observers, especially those sympathetic to the state of Israel, this speech nourished a geographical imagination based on the notion that Israel faces a genuine threat and is surrounded by neighbours determined to end its existence. For others less sympathetic to Israel, including elements within Iran, the speech was interpreted as a sign of geopolitical bravado – here was a political leader determined to stand up for the Palestinians and confront the geopolitical ambitions of Israel in the West Bank and southern Lebanon as well as American hegemonic ambitions in the region.

The link between the pronouncements of political leaders and their audiences (intended or otherwise) is an important component of our examination of geopolitics. I will use the term *popular geopolitics* in order to convey a sense of how images and representations of global political geographies circulate within and beyond national political cultures. There are two aspects to be considered – first, the manner in which political life is fused with the mass media and, second, the different kind of media involved in producing and circulating images of global politics whether it be television, radio, and/or the internet.

Structure of this book

The second chapter investigates the intellectual history associated with geopolitics. Despite the fact that most people using the term in newspaper, television reports, and/or the internet have no appreciation of its history, the ideas associated with geopolitics have changed over time. Engagement with this intellectual field differs markedly in the United States compared to Latin America, Germany, and Japan. The alleged connections between German geopolitics and Nazism were absolutely pivotal in shaping subsequent engagements. For example, very few scholars in either the United States or for that matter in the Soviet Union used the term geopolitics for nearly 40 years following the defeat of Nazi Germany in 1945. Why? They feared that they would in turn be accused of harbouring Nazi sympathies and ambitions.

Chapter 3 engages with the intersection between territory, resources, and flows. The dominant geopolitical architecture is an international system based on territorial states, exclusive jurisdictions, and national boundaries. However, geographical scale also matters because people and places are linked to one another from the local, to the national and regional, and finally to the global. While territory and resources such as oil deposits and water sources matter, so do flows – of people, ideas, goods, fuel, and money. Flows of the aforementioned can be welcomed, ignored and/or feared. In January 2006, the populace of Ukraine discovered what it is like when gas flows stop and thus houses are no longer heated. As the main supplier of gas to European customers, Russia holds considerable potential to wield influence, cajole, and bully. Sometimes governments and citizens do not appreciate the scale and significance of particular patterns of movement. In 2006, the British government admitted that it had no real idea quite how large the flow of illegal immigrants was to the United Kingdom. Alternatively, governments can struggle to manage the mobility of others. In the summer of 2006, Israel's superior military forces failed to root out and destroy the highly mobile and well-hidden combatants attached to Hezbollah in southern Lebanon.

Chapter 4 considers the relationship between geopolitics and identity. One persistent element embedded in the images and visions associated with the geographies of global politics is reference to self and others. When President Reagan described the Soviet Union as the 'evil empire', he was clear in his own mind that the United States was a force for good. As a former Hollywood actor, he might not have used the term 'a good empire' but anyone familiar with the Star Wars films would have appreciated the notion that the Soviet Union was part of 'the dark side'. The Soviet leader was the proverbial Darth Vader. The role of the other (in this case the Soviet Union) was a vitally important element in American self-understandings. It not only helped to identify a prevalent danger but also reinforced the self-identity of the United States as a force for good. As Michael Savage, a conservative talkshow host, told his listeners on 'The Savage Nation' in 2003 – "We are the good ones and they, the Arabs, are the evil ones'. His show enjoys a listening audience of 8 million and is syndicated to over 370 radio stations in the United States.

In practice these kinds of moral geographies were not always so clear cut – the Soviet Union was seen by many as a liberating force and communist utopia and the United States was considered to be an 'evil empire' by others. As I was reliably informed by a Lebanese man while sitting in a café in the centre of Beirut, America remains the 'Great Satan'. He made that observation to me in July 2003 at the same time as we shared views on Hollywood and American music, which my companion greatly enjoyed. I would be surprised if his view had changed of America's geopolitical presence given events in the summer of 2006, which witnessed the destruction of the city by Israeli bombers and missiles (paid for by American foreign aid).

The final two chapters consider various elements of what I have already labelled popular geopolitics. Chapter 5 investigates the role and significance of maps and mapping. Since its formal inception as a term in the 1890s, geopolitical writers have presented their maps of the world as definitive and/or enlightening, while often being oblivious to their own political and cultural prejudices. Maps can overemphasize some places over others and they can deliberately mislead and/or distort via omission or colour coding. German maps in the 1920s and 1930s frequently depicted 'international Jewry' as an Octopus-like creature in an attempt to further besmirch the reputation of that particular community. Moreover, by exaggerating the power of international Jewry, the Nazis prepared the cultural and geographical ground for their subsequent murderous policies, which culminated in the Holocaust. While maps were clearly only one element, they helped to shape the geographical imaginations of ordinary Germans even if many were perfectly capable of resisting such cartographic and ideological propaganda. Tragically, it was insufficient to prevent genocide.

The final chapter expands upon our examination of maps with a wider consideration of films, magazines, television, the internet, and radio and the way in which they contribute to the circulation of geopolitical images and representations of territory, resources, and identity. Consider a film such as *Wag the Dog* (1997), a Hollywood comedy which features an American president engulfed in a sexual crisis on the eve of his re-election campaign. His advisers are desperate to find a foreign policy diversion and decide that a 'crisis' has emerged that threatens the security of the United States. The country imperilling the United States is said to be Albania. The advisers then hire a top Hollywood producer who manufactures a short film clip of a girl running away from a village desperate to escape her Albanian attackers. Within this farrago, US forces are apparently dispatched to tackle the threat posed by Albanian terrorists. Throughout the whole White House-inspired diversionary campaign, the US media and public opinion is depicted as gullible and easily manipulated by the alleged footage. The incumbent President's approval ratings soar as a consequence of his firm action regarding the Albanian threat.

While many film critics were swift to point to the real-world connections between President Clinton and his sexual peccadilloes and the subsequent 1999 airborne assault on Serbia by US/NATO forces, the effectiveness of the film also depends on the audience's response and credulity that Albania might harbour terrorists armed with a nuclear bomb. As a Muslim country located in a corner of Europe, other Europeans have frequently labelled Albania as claustrophobic, criminalized, and confusing. Interestingly, the Serbian authorities broadcast the film to domestic viewers in an attempt to discredit President Clinton's decision to attack Serbian forces and infrastructure in Kosovo and Serbia itself. Ironically, US–NATO forces were dispatched in order to prevent Serbian forces from implementing further attacks on the Kosovo community, which is predominantly Muslim. As President Clinton explained to American television viewers in March 1999:

> Take a look at this map. Kosovo is a small place, but it sits on a major fault line between Europe, Asia and the Middle East, at the meeting place of Islam and both the Western and orthodox branches of Christianity. To the south are our allies, Greece and Turkey; to the north, our new democratic allies in Central Europe. And all around Kosovo there are other small countries, struggling with their own economic and political challenges – countries that could be overwhelmed by a large, new wave of refugees from Kosovo. All the ingredients for a major war are there: ancient grievances, struggling democracies, and in the center of it all a dictator in Serbia who has done nothing since the Cold War ended but start new wars and pour gasoline on the flames of ethnic and religious division.

As with President Roosevelt in 1942, he urged viewers to look to their maps and try to understand the complex geopolitics of South-East Europe. Unfortunately for Clinton, more Americans were probably preoccupied with the Monica Lewinsky affair. Geopolitics, as this very short introduction shows, is not merely an academic pursuit but an activity that deserves further reflection precisely because it is an essential part of everyday life in the United States and elsewhere. It is indeed smart to think geopolitically.

Chapter 2
An intellectual poison?

Introduction

> **All words have histories and geographies and the term 'geopolitics' is no exception. Coined in 1899, by a Swedish political scientist named Rudolf Kjellen, the word 'geopolitics' had a twentieth century history that was intimately connected with the belligerent dramas of that century.**
>
> **(Gearóid Ó Tuathail, 2006)**

In 1954, Richard Hartshorne lambasted geopolitics as an intellectual poison. During the Second World War, he had worked in the Office of Strategic Services (the forerunner of the Central Intelligence Agency) and helped to generate geographical intelligence for the US military. He, like other geographical scholars before him such as Isaiah Bowman, found geopolitics to be intellectually fraudulent, ideologically suspect, and tainted by association with Nazism (and other variants of fascism including Italian and Japanese) and its associated policies of genocide, racism, spatial expansionism, and the domination of place. Given this damning indictment, it is perhaps not altogether surprising to learn that many geographers in the United States and elsewhere including the Soviet Union were unwilling to enter this intellectual terrain. Within 50 years of its formal inception, therefore, it stood condemned by a cabal of geographers and more importantly by writers contributing to widely read American periodicals such as *Reader's Digest*, *Life*, and *Newsweek*. To claim, therefore, that geopolitics has had an eventful intellectual history would be something of an understatement.

How had geopolitics first attracted such opprobrium? In November 1939, *Life* magazine published an article on the German geographer Karl Haushofer and described him as the German 'guru of geopolitics'. The article contended that geopolitics, as a scientific practice, not only gave Nazism a sense of strategic rationality but also invested National Socialism with a form of pseudo-spirituality. Both aspects were significant in shaping public and elite attitudes towards this subject matter. On the one hand, geopolitics was condemned as a fraudulent activity not worthy of serious scholarly attention but, on the other hand, the critics bestowed upon it extraordinary powers to strategize and visualize global territory and resources. The use of the term 'guru' was not, therefore, entirely innocent precisely because it conveyed a sense of Nazism being endowed with a supernatural spirit and wicked sense of purpose. By the fall of 1941, the *Reader's Digest* alerted readers to the fact that at least a 1,000 more scientists were intellectually armed and ready to bolster the geopolitical imagination of Hitler and the German *Volk* (people). Frederick Sondern, writing for mass audiences in the *Reader's Digest* as well as in *Current History*, described a shadowy Munich-based organization called the Institute for Geopolitics that was intent on informing Hitler's plans for world domination. According to the author, the atmosphere was febrile:

> The work of Major General Professor Dr Karl Haushofer and his Geopolitical Institute in Munich, with its 1000 scientists, technicians and spies [is causing great alarm] ... These men are unknown to the public, even in the Reich. But their ideas, their

charts, maps, statistics, information and plans have dictated Hitler's moves from the very beginning.

Such was the concern about this shadowy institute and the extraordinary powers attributed to German geopolitics that President Roosevelt commissioned a series of academic studies on the subject. While those experts were less convinced about the claim concerning 1,000 scientists and technicians in the service of Hitler, they concurred that geopolitics was providing intellectual muscle to the practices associated with German statecraft including invasion and mass murder. What made the accusation of complicity even more damning was that some of the leading authors such as Haushofer were closely connected to the Nazi regime. This crossover between the academy and the world of government was crucial in adding further credibility to the charge that geopolitics was ideologically bankrupt and morally suspect.

By the time the Second World War was over, geopolitics stood widely condemned as being the handmaiden of Nazism and a whole post-war generation of scholars and their textbooks on political geography simply decided to omit geopolitics from their discussions. When one American-based geographer Ladis Kristof (father of the *New York Times* columnist Nicholas Kristof) tried to resurrect the term in the United States in the early 1960s, he was castigated by his colleagues and damned for even mentioning the term geopolitics in print.

The origins of the 'science' of geopolitics

In order to understand the alarm and outrage felt by American critics during the 1940s and beyond, it is necessary to appreciate fully the genesis of geopolitics as an intellectual term. Coined in 1899, by a Swedish professor of political science, Rudolf Kjellen, it has often been taken to signify a hard-nosed or more realistic approach to international politics that lays particular emphasis on the role of territory and resources in shaping the condition of states. This 'science' of geopolitics posited 'laws' about international politics based on the 'facts' of global physical geography (the disposition of the continents and oceans, the division of states and empires into sea- and land-powers). Reacting against what he perceived to be an overly legalistic approach to states and their conflicts with one another, the introduction of scientific geopolitics in the academic and government-orientated worlds of the 1890s and 1900s was opportune. As a portmanteau adjective, geopolitics attracted interest because it hinted at novelty – it was intended to investigate the often unremarked upon geographical dimensions of states and their position within world politics. Kjellen later became a Conservative member of the Swedish Parliament and was well known for his trenchant views on Swedish nationalism and foreign policy designs.

The claim to novelty is a little misleading and it helps only in part to explain why geopolitics became an attractive term and vibrant intellectual concern throughout continental Europe. Was geopolitics a 20th century academic reformulation of more traditional forms of statecraft and state calculation, previously carried out in ministries of foreign affairs and ministries of war through the 18th and 19th centuries, rather than in university classrooms?

Sarah O'Hara and Mike Heffernan have shown how many of the ideas associated with this nascent geopolitics were foreshadowed by government documents and press speculation. While geopolitics arose in response to specific late 19th-century concerns, it perhaps reflected more an act of academic colonization (in an era of major university expansion in Britain and continental Europe) of an activity previously conducted outside the academy.

Three factors contributed to the establishment of geopolitics as a distinct subject. First, economic nationalism and trade protectionism was on the rise as imperial European states such as

Britain and France agonized over the shifting and increasingly interconnected nature of the global economy. The rise of the United States as a trading power created further unease amongst these European powers. Second, imperial powers pursued an aggressive search for new territories in Africa and elsewhere in the mid to late 19th century. While imperial accumulation was on the rise, European powers confronted each other over ownership and access to those colonial territories. Britain and France were embroiled in tense encounters in North Africa, and Britain and Russia continued to jostle and parry in Central Asia under the sobriquet of the 'Great Game'. The famous British geopolitical writer Halford Mackinder described the new era as post-Columbian in the sense that the era of European exploration and colonization in the aftermath of Columbus's landing in the Americas in the 1490s was over. Ultimately, countries such as Britain and Germany engaged in rearmament, which provoked fears that conflict might materialize in Europe rather than simply erupt in faraway European held colonies. Finally, the growth of universities and the establishment of geography as an academic discipline created new opportunities for scholars to teach and research the subject. The alleged scientific status of geopolitics was important in establishing claims to intellectual legitimacy and policy relevance.

Invasion novels and geopolitical anxieties

The invasion novel was a historical genre which gained considerable popularity between the 1870s and 1914. One of the most recognizable was George Chesney's *The Battle of Dorking* (1871), a fictional account of an invasion of England by German armed forces. Others include Erskine Childer's *Riddle of the Sands* (1903) that featured two British men on a sailing holiday who happen to prevent a planned German invasion when they chance upon a secret fleet of invasion barges. By 1914, over 400 books had been published about

hypothetical invasions by overseas powers. Their popularity owes a great deal to the contemporary zeitgeist associated with Anglo-German rivalries, rearmament, and imperial competition in Africa and the Mediterranean. Public fears about 'foreigners' and German spy networks grew accordingly.

Invasion novels were also popular in Japan and emerged at a time when the Japanese confronted the Russians in 1904 for dominance of East Asia. In the United States, H. Irving Hancock wrote of an invasion by German forces and the occupation of the North-East Seaboard. American forces eventually repel the attackers.

The role of the United States in terms of economic and geopolitical influence further complicated these early geopolitical analyses of Europe and its imperial outposts. As contemporary observers such as Fredrick Jackson Turner opined, the American frontier was in the process of 'closing' as continental expansion came to its natural culmination. In the late 1890s, in the aftermath of the purchase of Alaska from Russia in the 1860s, the American Empire encapsulated the territories of Cuba, the Philippines, and Puerto Rico. Admiral Thomas Mahan, in his *The Influence of Sea Power upon History 1660–1783* (1898), offered some sobering advice to the then Theodore Roosevelt administration. As a one-time President of the Naval War College, he was well placed to contribute to American strategic thinking. Looking back at Anglo-French naval rivalry in the 17th and 18th centuries, Mahan recommended that the acquisition of naval power was the single most important factor in determining a nation's geopolitical power. Sea power was the 'handmaiden of expansion' and an expansionist United States would need to be able not only to project its power across the vast Atlantic and Pacific Oceans but also to have the capacity to deter and/or defeat any rivals.
The main threat, according to Mahan, lay with the German and

Russian Empires and their maritime ambitions. His work was later to be translated and read with great enthusiasm in Germany and played a part in shaping German geopolitical thinking in the 1920s and 1930s, especially in the development of pan-regional theorizing.

The writings of Kjellen, however, initially attracted swift attention from German scholars who explored in detail the relationship between politics and geography at a variety of geographical scales. In part, this movement of ideas owes much to geographical proximity and the interchange between German and Scandinavian scholars. German writers were, like Kjellen, deeply interested in conceptualizing the state according to its territorial and resource needs. Informed by variants of social Darwinism, the struggle of states and their human creators was emphasized, as was the need to secure the 'fittest' states and peoples. According to Fredrick Ratzel, Professor of Geography at the University of Leipzig, the state should be conceptualized as a super-organism, which existed in a world characterized by struggle and uncertainty. Trained in the natural sciences and conversant with the intellectual legacy associated with Charles Darwin and Jean Baptiste de Lamarck, Ratzel believed that the state was a geopolitical force rooted in and shaped by the natural environment. In order to prosper let alone survive in these testing circumstances, states needed to acquire territory and resources.

In his book, *The Sea as a Source of the Greatness of a People* (1901), Ratzel identified both the land and sea as providing opportunities and physical pathways for territorial expansion and eventual consolidation. A strong and successful state would never be satisfied by existing limits and would seek to expand territorially and secure 'living space'. Rival states would also seek such spaces so, according to Ratzel, any state seeking to expand would be engaged in a ceaseless cycle of growth and decline. The search for living space was in effect a fundamental and unchangeable geopolitical law – quite literally a fact of life on earth. He was, unsurprisingly, a passionate advocate of a German Empire and for a strong navy capable of protecting its overseas interests.

For many other writers as well, Germany's geographical location and historical experience at the centre of Europe was both a blessing and a curse – it had the potential to dominate the European continent but was also a victim of territorial loss and misfortune. Germany was, as Michael Korinman noted in 1990, 'a land of geographers', with some of the first established university faculties dedicated to teaching geography. On the eve of the First World War, German geographers such as Naumann and Partsch advocated a German alliance with the Austro-Hungarian Empire and a strong naval presence in order to expand its commercial objectives and territorial portfolio. With defeat in 1918 came the crushing realization that those ambitions were not likely to be achieved in the near future. The 1919 Peace Conference and the devastating financial and territorial settlement contained within the Treaty of Versailles sowed the seeds of resentment. When in the inter-war period, the ideas of Ratzel were resurrected, geographers in France such as Paul Vidal de la Blache worried that these ideas concerning the state as a super-organism could be deployed to justify a resurgent Germany, determined to extract revenge for its earlier territorial and ethnic dismemberment.

Elsewhere in Europe, geographers and military officers were engaging with geopolitical ideas and relating them to a broader discussion on colonialism, national regeneration, and imperial mission. In Portugal, for instance, the emergence of Salazar's regime in the early 1930s precipitated public displays and engagements with Portugal's mission in regard to the wider Portuguese-speaking world. In Italy, the new journal *Geopolitica* was created in order to facilitate further discussion over Italian geopolitical ambitions in the Mediterranean and Africa. In both countries, new maps were circulated in school textbooks and public murals with the purpose of instructing citizens about the geographical aspirations of these countries. In Spain, geopolitical discussion concentrated on Spanish colonial ambitions in North Africa and the government was anxious to project military power accordingly. Unlike Germany, Iberian geopolitical engagements were primarily preoccupied with colonial territories rather than reshaping the map of continental Europe.

When fears concerning a German military renaissance proved justifiable, the British geopolitical writer Mackinder advocated a Midland Ocean Alliance with the United States in order to counter any possible alliance between a resurgent Germany and the new Soviet Union. Although suggested in 1924, it is often understood to be one of the earliest proposals for a strategic alliance, which was later to be initiated by the North Atlantic Treaty Organization in April 1949. Although West Germany was an important cold war ally of the United States and Britain in the late 1940s, inter-war German geopolitical discourse was preoccupied with German territorial growth and cultural hegemony.

Geopolitics and Nazism

The most controversial element in the 20th-century history of geopolitics comes with its alleged association with Nazism and Hitler's plans for global domination. The idea of a state being considered as a super-organism and moreover requiring 'living space' provided a dangerous if not wholly original backdrop to inter-war engagements with geopolitical ideas. For one thing, the notion of the state as an organism encouraged a view of the world that focused on how to preserve national self-interest in an ultra-competitive environment comprised of other rapacious states. Given the apparent stakes, the maintenance of the organism becomes critical and anything or anyone that threatens the healthy integrity of the state would need to be addressed with some vigour. Internally, therefore, those that control the state need to be vigilant. Externally, the health of the state is said to depend upon the relentless acquisition of territory and resources. Again this kind of thinking tends to promote a view of the world which inevitably cherishes a well-equipped military force ready and willing to act when the need arises (an idea that was to be taken up with great enthusiasm in other parts of the world particularly by post-1945 Latin American military regimes). It also promotes a moral detachment because these geopolitical writers are considered to be simply reporting back on certain geographical realities that are removed from social and political intervention.

Geopolitics tries to give a scientific and reasoned explanation of the life of these super-beings who, with unrelenting activity on earth, are born, develop and die, a cycle during which they show all kinds of appetites and a powerful instinct for conservation. They are as sensible and rational beings as men.

(Late Chilean dictator and former Professor of Geopolitics, Augusto Pinochet, *Geopolitica*, 1968)

Critics have contended that Nazis such as Rudolf Hess and even Adolf Hitler deployed geopolitical insights and perspectives in order to promote and legitimate German expansionism in the 1930s and 1940s at the murderous expense of ethnic communities within Germany (the Jewish being the most obvious) and near neighbours such as Poland and Czechoslovakia. This association between geopolitics and Nazism remains much contested and relies in part on guilt by association. The notion of association is significant – it refers both to an intellectual connection but more significantly to a personal bond between some leading German geographers and highly placed Nazis.

At the heart of this accusation concerning the intellectual and political connections between geopolitics and Nazism lie the writings and social networks of Professor Karl Haushofer. Born in 1869, he entered the German army and finally retired in 1919 with the rank of major general. During his period of military service, he was sent to Japan in order to study their armed forces. Whilst on secondment (1908–10), Haushofer learnt Japanese and developed a keen interest in that country's culture. His interactions with Japanese military officers and geographers was critical in facilitating the emergence of Japanese geopolitical institutes such as the Japan Association for Geopolitics and the Geopolitics School at the University of Kyoto in the 1920s and 1930s. He was and remains a towering intellectual influence in the development of geopolitics not just in Germany and Japan but also in South America where his work was translated into Spanish and Portuguese and used extensively by the armed forces of countries such as Argentina, Brazil, and Chile.

After his retirement from the army, Haushofer became a Professor of Geography at the University of Munich and initiated the publication of the Journal of Geopolitics (*Zeitschrift für Geopolitik*) in the mid-1920s. As with his predecessor Ratzel, Haushofer believed that German survival would depend upon a clear-headed appreciation of the geographical realities of world politics. If the state was to prosper rather than just survive, the acquisition of 'living space', particularly in the East, was vital and moreover achievable with the help of potential allies such as Italy and Japan. An accommodation with the Soviet Union was also, in the short to medium term, wise because it would enable both countries to consolidate their respective positions on the Euro-Asian landmass. In order for Germany to prosper, its leadership would need, he believed, to consider carefully five essential elements, which lay at the heart of a state's design for world power: physical location, resources, territory, morphology, and population. If Germany were to be a 'space-hopping' state rather than 'space-bound', it would need to understand and act upon its territorial and resource potential.

Haushofer also promoted the idea of a theory of pan-regions, which posited that Germany and other powerful states such as Japan should develop their own economic and geographical hinterlands free from interference with one another. In order for Germany to dominate part of the Euro-Asian landmass, an accommodation with the Soviet Union was essential, as was a modus operandi with Britain, which was understood to be in control of Africa. Haushofer's prime geographical orientation was towards the East and he was an enthusiastic supporter of plans to develop a Berlin–Baghdad railway, which would enable Germany to project its influence in the Middle East and Central Asia. If developed, the railway would have facilitated access to oil supplies and (the British feared) a platform to disrupt trade to and from Asia. While the 1919 Peace Conference terminated German ambitions to pursue such a scheme, his idea of pan-regions appealed to both traditional eastward-looking nationalists and industrialists eager to exploit the raw materials held in German colonies outside Europe.

While his ideas have been seen as intellectually underpinning Hitler's project of spatial expansionism and genocidal violence, critics contended (especially American observers in the 1940s) that these ideas mattered because of Haushofer's friendship with Rudolf Hess and his high-level involvement in German-Japanese negotiations in the 1930s and 1940s. Before his appointment as Hitler's private secretary and later deputy in the Nazi party, Hess was a student of Haushofer at the University of Munich. In his work, *Mein Kampf*, Hitler evokes terms such as living space (*Lebensraum*) to expound upon his belief that Germany needed to reverse the 1919 Treaty of Versailles and seek a new geographical destiny involving Central and Eastern Europe.

There is, however, a critical difference between the two men. Unlike Haushofer who was largely preoccupied with spatial relationships and the organic state, Hitler placed a far greater emphasis on the role of people (in his case the Aryan race) in determining the course of history and geography. In other words, Hitler's obsession with race and his hatred of German and European Jewry did not find any intellectual inspiration from the writings of Haushofer. If the two agreed on anything, it was that the German state was a super-organism that needed 'living space' and associated territorial outlets. Despite his connections with Nazi officials, Haushofer's influence was on the wane by the late 1930s and early 1940s. He neither believed, as many Nazis did, that an international cabal of Jews and Communists was plotting to take over the world nor endorsed Hitler's obsession with the undue influence of German Jewry on the national welfare of Germany itself.

By 1941–2, German émigré intellectuals such as Hans Weigert, Andreas Dorpalen, Andrew Gyorgy, and Robert Strausz-Hupe had firmly implanted in the American imagination that German *Geopolitik* was Nazism's scientific partner in crime. Just as Haushofer was accused of being the evil genius behind the Nazi menace, his position and influence was, as we have noted, actually in decline. Furthermore, he thought that the German invasion of the Soviet Union in 1941 was strategically misguided and his close relationship with Rudolf Hess became a liability when it was discovered that Hess had secretly flown to Scotland in the same year in an attempt to seek peace with Britain. While the origins of Hess's mission are still unclear, it marked a turning point in the alleged influence of German geopolitical thinking on Hitler and his associates.

Haushofer committed suicide in 1946 after learning that his son Albrecht had been executed in April 1945 for his part in the bomb plot to kill Hitler in July 1944. One person who discussed geopolitical ideas with Karl Haushofer was the American colonel and Jesuit priest, Father Edmund Walsh. Interested in German and Soviet geopolitical writings, Walsh determined that Haushofer should not be indicted for war crimes even if he, like those aforementioned German émigré writers, was convinced that

Haushofer was the 'brains-trust' of Hitler. As he noted in his 1948 book *Total Power*,

> the interrelation of cause and effect could no longer be disguised, as one invasion after another followed the broad pattern so long and so openly expounded in the writings and teachings of the master geopolitician.

Given Walsh's detailed interrogation of Haushofer in 1945, his academic judgment carried some considerable weight but even he stopped short of blaming Haushofer's intellectual corpus and personal relationships for Hitler's racist and expansionist policies.

Post-war decline in the United States

Having earned damnation and opprobrium from distinguished observers such as Edmund Walsh, who became the Dean of the United States Foreign Service at Georgetown University, it is not surprising that the reputation of geopolitics was in tatters. A new generation of American political geographers spurned the term and instead concentrated on developing political geography, which was carefully distinguished as intellectually objective and less deterministic with regard to the influence of environmental factors on the behaviour of states. In his important review of post-war Anglophone geopolitics, Leslie Hepple contends that the term 'geopolitics' dropped out of circulation of American political and popular life between 1945 and 1970. With very few exceptions, such as the Czech-born Professor of Sociology at the University of Bridgeport, Joseph Roucek, who published prolifically in academic and popular journals on topics such as the geopolitics of the United States or Antarctica, the term was studiously avoided. What is striking about all Roucek's articles containing the title 'geopolitics' is that he shows little to no interest in exploring the conceptual terrain occupied by the subject. For him, geopolitics is a useful shorthand (and apparently self-evident) term to highlight the significance of territory and resources.

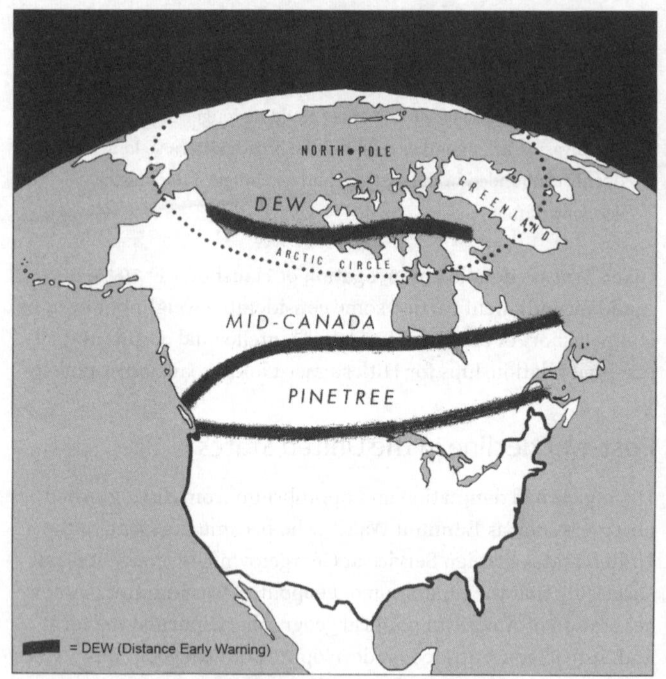

4. Listening and watching during the cold war

Despite Roucek's spirited adoption, very few others were willing to employ a term so apparently tainted by an association with Nazism. This did not mean, however, that geographers abandoned their interest in the global political map. Geographers such as Nicholas Spykman (1893–1943) and later Saul Cohen recognized that the onset of the cold war meant it was more important than ever before to understand the territorial and ideological nature of the struggle between the Soviet Union and the United States. In his pioneering work, *Geography and Politics in a Divided World* (1963), Cohen followed up an interest in Spykman's understanding of a patently fractured world.

If Spykman drew attention to what he called the rimlands of Eastern Europe, the Middle East, and South and South-East Europe, Cohen's later work focused on so-called shatterbelts and attempted to explain where the superpowers were likely to be locked into conflicts over territory, resources, and access. The geographical regions closest to the Soviet Union and later China were seen as the main battlegrounds of the cold war. Conflict and tension in Berlin, South-East Europe, the Middle East, Korea, and Vietnam seemed to add credence to that geographical view even if the high-profile Cuban missile crisis of 1962 demonstrated that the United States was extremely sensitive about the geographically proximate Caribbean basin.

Ironically, just as the term geopolitics was losing its credibility in the United States, Japan, Britain, and other parts of Europe, an argument emerged that American cold war strategy was implicitly inspired by geopolitical ideas. The National Security Council's NSC-68 document, delivered to President Truman in April 1950, warned of the Soviet Union's plans for world domination and possible geographical strategies for achieving that fundamental aim. Although dismissive of the Third World and its geographical diversity, NSC 68 was later to be supplemented by the so-called domino theory that warned that the Third World was vulnerable to Soviet-backed expansionism. Within a decade of the formation of the North Atlantic Treaty Organization in 1949, the United States created security pacts in Australasia (1951), Central Asia (1955), and entered into bilateral security arrangements with Japan and South Korea.

The few American political geographers such as Cohen who did comment explicitly on the cold war and US strategy were in agreement with general aims such as the containment of the Soviet Union but anxious to highlight the tremendous diversity of the Third World. In the eagerness to understand the global ambitions of the Soviet Union, Cohen warned American readers that they should not underestimate the profound geographical, cultural, and political differences between the Middle East, on the one hand, and South Asia, on the other. American strategists, such as George Kennan who worked at the Department of State during the Truman administration, were, it was alleged, neglectful of those regional differences and NSC-68 was seen as geographically simplistic and overly concerned with representing the Soviet Union as a relentlessly expansionist threat from the East.

Geopolitical revival in the United States

Former Secretary of State Henry Kissinger is often credited with the revival of American interest in geopolitics even if his usage was far more informal than the turn-of-the-century exponents. Kissinger, as a German émigré and intellectual whose doctoral thesis had analysed 19th-century European geopolitical history, was not typical of Secretaries of States in the post-1945 period. He was an intellectual heavyweight in the Nixon administration and keen observer of the changing geopolitical condition of the cold war. The context of the time was critical – the cold war was entering a new phase of relative détente, even if the Soviet Union, the United States, and China were still suspicious of one another's motives and geopolitical ambitions. The United States was immersed in an increasingly unpopular conflict in Vietnam and Kissinger's use of the term geopolitics was in part an attempt to come to grips with a new strategic landscape. In the main, as Leslie Hepple has recorded, he uses the term to highlight the importance of global equilibrium and permanent national interests in a world characterized by a balance of power. Eager to promote a new relationship with China, he argued that Moscow's 'geopolitical ambitions' needed to be contained:

> Equilibrium was the name of the game. We did not seek to join China in a provocative confrontation with the Soviet Union. But we agreed on the necessity to curb Moscow's geopolitical ambitions.

Peking's challenge was polemical and philosophical; it opposed not only Moscow's geopolitical aspirations but also its ideological pre-eminence. We agreed on the necessity of thwarting the geopolitical ambitions, but we had reason to become involved in the ideological dispute.

While the United States strived to contain the Soviet Union, Kissinger believed that existing American foreign policy had been too eager to promote a military response to this dilemma. Instead what was required was, in an era of relative American military decline, an approach which was flexible and attentive to new political possibilities such as developing relations with other powers like China.

Although Kissinger's usage of the term geopolitics has been described as fuzzy and vague, it nonetheless according to some scholars repopularized the term within American political culture and led to renewed formal academic reflection on global strategy. In terms of popularity, geopolitics was reintroduced into discussions on cold war politics alongside a host of other subjects that sought to connect global and regional issues. While few authors possessed a detailed appreciation of the term's tortured intellectual history, it served as an apparently useful moniker to highlight the significance of geographical factors in shaping political and military developments. Other leading political figures such as President Carter's Polish-born National Security Adviser, Zbigniew Brzezinski, were keen advocates of geopolitics and used the term to signal their interest in projecting America's strategic interests in an era of mounting global tension and, for those who were later to be called neo-conservative intellectuals, cited remorseless Soviet expansionism. The decision to fund and support resistance to the Soviet occupation of Afghanistan from 1979 onwards was informed by a geopolitical belief that further expansion had to be contained even if it meant that the United States and its regional allies such as Pakistan supported proxies in order to resist Soviet forces. As many have noted, this decision had

5. **Henry Kissinger: *Time Life* cover, 10 June 1974**

important ramifications in terms of inspiring the creation of the Al-Qaeda terror network and producing battle-hardened veterans such as Osama bin Laden.

One of the most significant offshoots of this revival of geopolitics was the creation of the Committee on the Present Danger, which used geopolitics and other academic pursuits such as Sovietology (the study of Soviet government and society, sometimes described as 'Kremlin Watching') to contend that America had to be prepared to ditch policies of détente and balance of power in favour of a more aggressive approach which recognized that the Soviet Union was determined to extend its domination over the entire Euro-Asian landmass. Disappointed with the more dovish Carter administration, these intellectuals and academic commentators such as Colin Gray promoted a geopolitical world view, which was later to be adopted by the Reagan administration. American foreign policy arguably pursued Soviet-backed proxies in Central America and Africa and more forcefully supported anti-Soviet regimes throughout the Third World. If that meant, for instance, supporting Saddam Hussein's regime in Iraq and countless military regimes in Latin America then so be it. Short to medium range nuclear missiles were stationed in Britain and West Germany as part of NATO's attempt to dispel any Soviet attempts to expand their influence in Western and Central Europe.

By the mid-1980s, geopolitical discussions within the United States were primarily shaped by a group of scholars strongly influenced by political realism and a desire to maintain American power in the midst of the so-called second cold war following the collapse of détente. Geopolitics once more became a shorthand term for great power rivalries and signalled the importance of the United States pursuit of its own national interests in an anarchical world. United States foreign policy under Reagan was certainly more aggressive than under the Carter presidency and many intellectuals and policy makers associated with that administration were later to become members of the George H. W. Bush and George W. Bush administrations. Defense Secretary Donald Rumsfeld, infamously shook hands with Saddam Hussein in the early 1980s yet was later instrumental in planning and executing the invasion of Iraq in 2003 and his overthrow and subsequent execution in December 2006.

Towards a critical geopolitics

About the same time that certain policy intellectuals were revisiting the term geopolitics in the contest of the cold war, other writers were exploring a rather different conception of geopolitics. Later to be dubbed critical geopolitics, this approach was not realist in tone and outlook. As an approach to the study of international relations, realism has been highly significant, especially in the United States. It tends to assume that states inhabit a world which is anarchical because of an absence of a world government capable of restricting their actions. In the most basic forms of realism, self-interest and power projection are assumed as a consequence to be axiomatic. For many geopolitical writers, even if they do not refer to some of the high priests of realism such as E. H. Carr and Kenneth Waltz, they implicitly work with a model that is similar in outlook to many realists. For the Latin American generals preoccupied with their national security state in the 1960s and 1970s, the realist world view coincided well with a geopolitical imagination filled with dangers and threats from communist forces inside and outside the state.

For the critics of this kind of realist-inspired geopolitics, this jaundiced view of global politics is one-dimensional in the sense that it tends to overemphasize conflict and competition at the expense of cooperation and détente. The inter-state system has demonstrated a capacity, perhaps surprising to some observers, to collaborate and develop joint institutions, international law, and intergovernmental bodies such as the European Union and the United Nations. Moreover, a new generation of writers, inspired by different philosophical traditions, is sceptical of the claims of realist-inspired writers to simply 'tell it as it is'. In other words, far from presenting a disinterested world view of global politics, it is profoundly shaped by particular representational schemas, which in turn reflect linguistic and cultural conventions. It is perhaps unsurprising that realist inspired geopolitics has found a warm reception in the United States, where it is common for writers

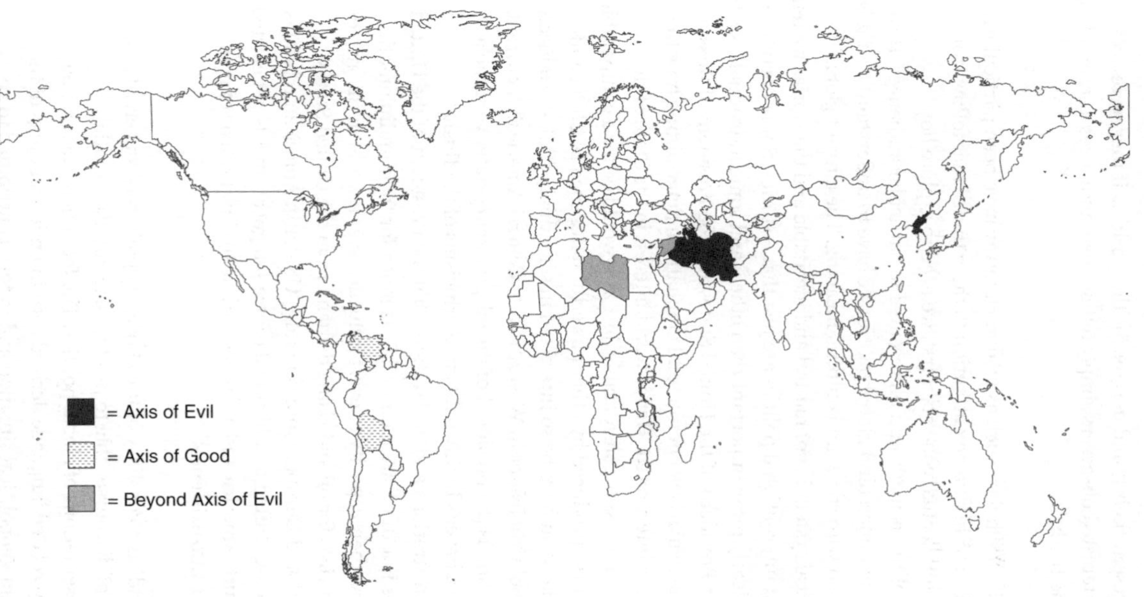

6. Axes of good and evil

to present their grand designs for the world as if they were disinterested observers simply telling their audiences a series of 'home truths'.

Feminist scholars such as Donna Haraway have been particularly significant in drawing attention to three things that follow from such intellectual conceits. First, we need to explore how geopolitics is made and represented to particular audiences. If we want to understand global politics we have to understand that it is imbued with social and cultural meaning. The current global political system is not natural and inevitable and the stories we tell about international politics are just that – stories. Some narratives are clearly more important than others and some individuals, such as the President of the United States and the President of Russia, are particularly vociferous and emphatic in determining how the world is interpreted. Hence world interest in the State of the Union address is considerable, just as it would be for a comparable discourse produced by other powerful states such as China and Russia. Would we be so interested in something similar produced by a political leader in West Africa or Central America? A current exception is the president of the oil-producing state, Venezuela. Hugo Chavez's highly publicized criticisms of the Bush administrations and declarations that the President of the United States is a 'devil' are memorable as much for their undiplomatic tone as their capacity to exert influence over a world in the grip of high prices for oil and rising demand from the United States, China, and Europe. More generally, US–Latin American relations are being shifted as additional centre-left governments get elected in South America and a new, according to Chavez, 'axis of good' comes into existence.

Second, as a corollary of the above, geopolitics is conceived as a form of discourse, able to produce and circulate spatial representations of global politics. The focus here was on how policy-related language derived certain understandings of the current geopolitical situation and in turn contributed to an identity politics, which was critical in securing the United States' sense of itself. In an era that was largely defined as both a battle of ideas and influence, the cold war lent itself to this kind of geographical focus – attention was given as much to certain imagined geographies as it was to the actual manifestations of the conflict in places such as Afghanistan and/or Central America. Those imagined geographies included frequent representations of the United States, under the Reagan administration, as the 'leader of the free world' and the Soviet Union as the evil empire hell-bent on imperilling Western civilization.

Third, global geopolitics is entangled with questions of gender and other factors such as race and class. The everyday experiences of women and children and the strategies that they have to adopt in order to cope with geopolitical and geo-economic processes and structures need to be recognized as fundamentally different to the experiences of many men irrespective of their geographical location. Concepts such as territory, borders, and scale take on a different meaning when considering war rape in Democratic Republic of the Congo compared to the immigration of young men from North Africa to Southern Europe. If the global political boundaries are more porous to capital than to people, they are also more porous in general to men as opposed to women. As Cynthia Enloe has concluded, global geopolitics needs to be linked to the everyday geographies of gender relations in order to better understand the differential impact of national boundaries, security, conflict, and migration.

In order to understand better how geopolitics works, critical geopolitical writers have proposed a threefold division – formal, practical, and popular. The formal is concerned with the subject matter of this chapter. How do academics and commentators self-consciously invoke an intellectual tradition associated with geopolitics? Practical geopolitics refers to the policy-orientated geographical templates used by political leaders such as President Bush as they represent global politics. Finally, popular geopolitics

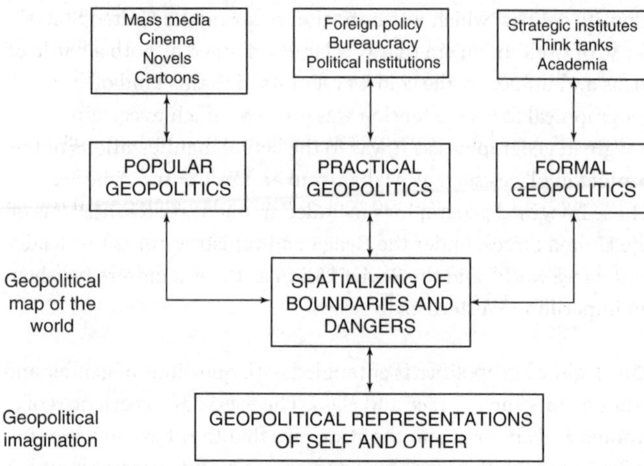

7. Formal, practical, and popular geopolitics

includes the role of the media and other forms of popular culture, which citizens use to make sense of events in their own locale, country, region, and the wider world. All three forms are interconnected as academic writers and journalists routinely share ideas and discourses with one another and both groups have regular contacts with government officials and organizations. They are also immersed in the media and popular culture. Geopolitical frameworks can help both individuals and groups make sense of the world for themselves and a wider public. Phrases such as 'axis of evil' attract attention precisely because they are designed to simplify world politics and locate friends and enemies. Presidents and prime ministers might use them initially (sometimes injudiciously) but these kinds of grand spatial abstractions provoke and promote discussions amongst journalists, pundits, and reading and listening public audiences.

The political geographer, Gearóid Ó Tuathail, has argued that this tripartite schema resides within a geopolitical culture, which shapes a state's encounter with the world. Britain's physical location on the edge of Europe, while it should not be seen as predetermining particular policy outcomes such as commitment to the European integrative process, clearly has been significant in shaping cultural interpretations of geographical location. Also significant have been wartime experiences when Britain was forced to defend its national territories from German forces, including bombing raids and rocket attacks associated with the Blitz. Hence the shock and humiliation felt by some politicians such as Prime Minister Margaret Thatcher when the news broke that the Falkland Islands had been invaded by Argentina in April 1982. Political leaders and journalists rapidly invoked parallels with the Second World War in an attempt to explain the dispatch of a naval taskforce, which ultimately prevailed against the Argentine forces in June 1982. During the conflict itself, Thatcher ensured that Britain had the support of the United States and this 'special relationship' was critical in ensuring access to weaponry and satellite information about Argentine military deployments. As with Prime Minister Blair over Iraq, Thatcher placed considerable importance on the Anglo-American relationship at the expense of a geopolitical tradition based on European Britain.

Britain's four geopolitical traditions

1. **Little England/Britain.**
2. **Cosmopolitan Britain.**
3. **European Britain.**
4. **American Britain.**

(Adapted from Timothy Garton Ash, *Free World*, 2004)

Likewise, if we wished to understand better Russian geopolitical culture, we would need to appreciate, as the geographer Graham Smith noted, how political leaders and journalists have invoked three separate geopolitical traditions. First, the notion that Russia is a part of Europe and that the country needs to embrace Western models of social and economic development. Second, Russia is a distinctive Euro-Asian territory, with its own particular form of state and society. Finally, Russia, like Britain, is a 'bridge', in this case between Europe and Asia. At certain times, a particular geopolitical tradition might be dominant over others, such as President Bush's determination to pursue a geopolitical vision of a global United States, which is concerned with American hegemony and ability to project power in order to secure the national interest.

This kind of appreciation of geopolitics as a broader cultural enterprise is not without precedent, however. Throughout the intellectual history of geopolitics, there are examples of individuals and groups committed to different forms of cultural and historical analysis, such as those found in critical geopolitics today. The work of Yves Lacoste and his Parisian colleagues deserves some mention because Lacoste was one of the first to really consider how geopolitics was a form of political and strategic knowledge. He penned a book in 1976, with the arresting English-language title of *Geography is Above All, Concerned with the Making of War*, which followed an earlier interest in the manner American military planners used geographical knowledge of North Vietnam to target rivers and jungles in order to inflict ecocide (i.e. the deliberate destruction of local ecosystems in order to weaken adversaries) on the local population. He also examined the geopolitical theories of President Pinochet of Chile who was a former Professor of Geopolitics at the Chilean War College in the 1960s. The latter even penned a tome on geopolitics in which he advocated the view of the state as a super-organism and arguably put theory into practice when he helped to remove the socialist government of Salvador Allende on 11 September 1973. American support was judged to be critical and Henry Kissinger, then Secretary of State, once noted with reference to Chile that

> [I] don't see why we need to stand by and watch a country go communist due to the irresponsibility of its people. The issues are much too important for the Chilean voters to be left to decide for themselves.

Lacoste argued that geopolitical writers needed to be more self-critical and play their part in unmasking how geopolitics was implicated with expressions of militarism and state power. His journal *Herodote* continues to be the largest circulation geography journal in the French-speaking world and publishes critical analyses of contemporary events such as the Global War on Terror. Although Lacoste once noted that it was 'not in good taste to make reference to geopolitics', he has advocated an approach to the subject which is informed by critical regional analysis (i.e. demonstrating an appreciation for local and regional differences) and an understanding of the connections between geographical knowledge and political practice.

If geopolitics is worthy of further critical reflection, it is precisely because it has attracted a great deal of academic and popular attention, often with little appreciation of its controversial intellectual history. Presidents, prime ministers, and pundits love the term. It purports to deal with dangers, threats, space, and power. It helps to explain the world in simple terms – geographical templates such as the Third World often appear to have a reassuring solidity. It also empowers users to make predictions about the future direction of global politics. Journalists and academic commentators frequently invoke geopolitics when they wish to promote the next major development, whether it is the clash of civilizations, the rise of China, the End of History (and Geography), the new American Century, or the notion that Americans and Europeans are destined to misunderstand one another because they occupy different geopolitical universes.

Conclusions

The final part of our brief overview of geopolitics as an intellectual term has turned again to the United States and the English-speaking world. As I have indicated in earlier sections, this account needs to be complemented with a word of caution. The story presented here might be characterized as one of emergence, notoriety, decline, and revival. However, if this chapter had concentrated on the experiences of South America, a very different story would have emerged. For one thing, we would not have had to concern ourselves to the same degree with the alleged stigma of Nazism. In places such as the military academies of Argentina, Brazil, Chile, and Paraguay, which enjoyed a close relationship with the Italian and German militaries, military officers continued to teach and publish in the field of geopolitics throughout the post-1945 period. German geopolitical writings were translated into Spanish and Portuguese at a time when American geographers were urging their peers to avoid the term and its abhorrent connotations. In a continent dominated by military regimes for much of the cold war period, geopolitics flourished without much formal concern about connections to Nazism and associated policies of spatial expansionism and the domination of place.

Scholars in the Soviet Union who still considered geopolitics to be ideologically tainted with Nazism did not welcome this revival of interest, especially in the 1980s. While there is far more formal engagement with the term in post-Soviet Russia, memories of the Second World War and associated heavy Soviet losses of life played a part in shaping academic reactions to this new engagement of interest in North America and Western Europe. Fifty years later, this stigma appears to have been lifted and a new generation of mainly right-wing Russian and others such as Uzbek commentators have used earlier geopolitical writers such as Halford Mackinder in particular to consider their countries' geopolitical destinies. One area of mounting interest is the strategic significance of Central Asia and the emergence of a so-called 'Great Game' between the United States, China, and Russia. The United States and China seek, much to the alarm of Russia, to extend their military and resource investments in a region characterized by largely untapped oil and natural gas resources in the Caspian Sea.

The final point to reiterate, apart from geopolitics's varied intellectual history is that the last section on critical geopolitics should not be misunderstood. Only a small group of scholars in the United States and elsewhere would describe themselves as critical geopolitical scholars. In most countries, including the United States, most people using the term geopolitics have little interest in understanding that contorted intellectual history. Moreover, they use geopolitics as a shorthand term usually intended to invest their work with a kind of rugged respectability and willingness to ponder and report upon the grim geographical realities of world politics. Authors such as the well known American commentator Thomas Barnett often claim, in a manner reminiscent of earlier geopolitical writers, an ability to see the world and to make confident predictions about its future composition, usually for the benefit of one particular country as opposed to others. Critical geopolitical writers aim to scrutinize those claims and, where appropriate, suggest other geographical ways of representing and understanding the world. This might include, for instance, laying emphasis on the human security and the gendered nature of global geopolitics, which often means that women and children are more vulnerable and exposed to geopolitical violence and geo-economic inequalities. Often this work attempts to liberate populations from oppressive geopolitical structures and promotes geographical understandings of a more equal world. This includes, for instance, laying greater emphasis on the gendered nature of global politics and geo-economic inequalities in the world trade system.

Chapter 3
Geopolitical architectures

In recent years, the most important shorthand term used by political leaders, journalists, and academic commentators to describe and explain global political and economic change has been globalization. Since the 1980s, it has become virtually hegemonic in academic and policy-making circles and was readily embraced by President Bill Clinton in the 1990s, for example. Within those varied discussions, globalization was frequently assumed to be transforming the world around us, as governments and agencies such as the World Trade Organization, the United Nations, and the International Monetary Fund either encouraged or struggled to handle the apparent pace of change. As a consequence, territory and international borders appeared less significant in shaping human affairs – some commentators such as Richard O'Brien even referred to the 'End of Geography'. Rather than subscribe to that view, this chapter will illustrate how globalization coexists with a geopolitical architecture involving states and other non-state bodies, which far from eroding the significance of borders and territory are contributing to dynamic reconfigurations. In the post-cold war era, the way we organize our world, define the roles and responsibilities of organizations such as the United Nations and the conduct of states has been subjected to intense scrutiny.

> **When Communism failed, the Berlin Wall fell, and the economy became truly global, America and other wealthy nations reaped very big benefits. But I think very few people had thought through the full implications of the new world in which we found ourselves. A world characterized not just by a global economy, but also by a global information society. When I took the oath of office as President on January the 20th, 1993, there were only 50 sites on the World Wide Web. When I left office, there were over 350 million and rising. Today, they're probably somewhere around 500 million.**
>
> **(Bill Clinton, University of California, Jan 2002)**

But what is globalization? The term refers to the movement of people, ideas, technology, and goods from place to place with corresponding implications for human relations. Since the 15th and 16th centuries, these flows have become progressively more intense, often with severe implications for native populations in what were later to be described as the First, Second, and Third Worlds. The Dutch, Portuguese, Spanish, British, and French were at the forefront of this global enterprise and the 'colonial encounter' initiated a global trade in commodities and people including slaves. Global entities such as the Dutch East India Company, assisted by their imperial sponsors, helped to construct and administer these trading networks. By the 19th century, a new continental power, the United States, began to make its presence felt in terms of its flows of people, goods, and ideas alongside territorial acquisition in the Pacific Ocean and the Caribbean. As the global economy further materialized in the same period, the need for international coordination increased and the 1884 International Meridian Conference established Greenwich as the Prime Meridian and thus facilitated a new world map of agreed-upon time zones. The 20th century bore witness to even greater forms of social, political, and cultural connectivity due to

8. The Dutch East India Company built their headquarters at Batavia, Jakarta, Indonesia

the advances in aviation, automobiles, and containerization. At its end, as the international system widened and deepened, geography in the sense of physical space no longer seemed to matter. For the journalist Thomas Friedman, the year 2000 was the high water mark of globalization as software technology and the internet brought people and objects ever closer together.

While the 'End of Geography', like the 'End of History', has been much proclaimed, the varied geographies of globalization have arguably highlighted the significance of borders, distance, interconnection, and responsibilities. Since the 17th century, European states and later others such as the United States have sought actively to manage the relationship between national territories and accompanying flows of people, goods, ideas, and money. The 19th century, as Gerrit Gong has noted, heralded the establishment of 'standards of civilization' that enabled European states to determine the current and future shape of the international system and the criteria by which new states achieved legal recognition via a form of 'earned sovereignty'. The latter in its many and varied guises is an essential element of globalization as it helps to provide 'rules' and 'expectations' for the global order. The United States, as a great power, has in the recent past been at the forefront of establishing such an international legal order. It was instrumental in creating post-1945 institutions such as the United Nations and the 1948 Universal Declaration of Human Rights. In the United Nations Charter, for instance, states accept that the Security Council has the right to determine what constitutes threats to international peace and security and that states must comply with particular resolutions relating to these. More generally, there has been a gulf between legal sovereignty and *de facto* sovereignty in the sense that 'sovereignty' has been abused, divided, and shared.

As has become alarmingly clear in recent years, the George W. Bush administration (2001–9) has been widely judged to be indifferent to these kinds of constraining structures as it seeks to control and indeed eradicate flows of terrorists and their funding. While Bush's policies are correlated with a lack of additional terror events within the United States, it has failed to prevent other flows and networks from inflicting terrible losses of life and infrastructure in the Middle East and Central Asia. Importantly, the Bush administration has also sought to reterritorialize the world, often in the form of simplistic spatial frameworks such as the 'axis of evil'. One way, therefore, of responding to these flows of people, money, and objects is to try to 'freeze' geographical space in the hope of promoting a sense of geopolitical stability and cultural reassurance.

The term *geopolitical architecture* is used to describe the ways in which states and non-state organizations access, manage, and regulate the intersection of territories and flows and in so doing establish borders between inside/outside, citizen/alien, and domestic/international. Governments, for instance, invest greatly in the regulation of borders as they provide the entry/exit point into a national territory. Such border controls also become a significant element in demonstrating effective sovereignty. In the summer of 2006, the British government introduced new security measures at all airports because a plot to blow up a number of planes was uncovered. This security alert acted as a pretext for new measures designed to increase the monitoring and surveillance of passengers seeking to enter and/or depart the UK. While it is too early to judge its effectiveness, controlling the mobility of passengers in a tightly defined space is just one of the more obvious everyday manifestations of a geopolitical architecture.

Concepts and processes associated with globalization, sovereignty, and international law therefore shape the geopolitical architecture of global politics. The international system, based on states and accompanying principles such as exclusive sovereignty and non-intervention, changes greatly over time and space. In order to understand those shifts and the implications for geopolitical theorizing, we need to consider two fundamental subjects – first, the term sovereignty and how it informs the activities of the state and, second, the geopolitical architecture of the 20th century, which witnessed the emergence of more states than ever before and greater pressures from a variety of state and non-state organizations. Reference to the political dimensions of globalization will be an important part of this discussion and interested readers should, of course, consult the excellent discussion of the topic by Manfred Steger and his accompanying 'Very Short Introduction'.

Geopolitics of national sovereignty and the international system

The ideas and practices associated with sovereignty are critical in shaping the prevailing geopolitical architecture based on states, borders, and national territories. As Stephen Krasner has noted, national governments, while endorsing the importance of sovereignty, have frequently violated those ideas and principles as incorporated into the founding charter of the United Nations. The United States invasion of Iraq in 2003 serves as a recent illustration of that willingness to violate the national sovereignty of another country while at the same time stressing the significance of territorial integrity. But there are many others we could cite such as Saddam Hussein's invasion of Kuwait in August 1990 and the Soviet invasion of Afghanistan in 1979. Sometimes governments willingly allow their national sovereignty to be violated by encouraging certain flows of investment, skilled people, and ideas. Since the enlargement of the European Union, the British government has encouraged labour migration from countries such as Poland and Slovakia. In other cases, governments may appeal for humanitarian and/or military intervention when faced with overwhelming evidence of human rights violation and suffering. The situation facing the Bosnian government in 1992 provides a tragic example in a country then confronted by Serbian military aggression. Appeals to the European Union and the United States failed until 1995 to catalyse a sufficiently large military force (or to lift an arms embargo) determined to end the violation of Bosnian national territory and the communities therein. Since then the Dayton Peace Plan designed for Bosnia has been monitored by the United Nations appointed High Representative, which in the past has included the British politician Lord Ashdown.

In thinking about sovereignty, it is helpful to distinguish four different types of interpretation. First, commentators frequently refer to the international legal manifestations of sovereignty in the form of membership of the United Nations, the ability to negotiate and ratify treaties alongside the general business associated with diplomacy. At the heart of these activities is the notion that states recognize other states and therefore accept that they have an inherent capacity to conduct *international* relations. Even if other governments detest a state and its political leadership, that basic recognition is fundamental. In the weeks and months leading up

9. Mostar, Bosnia: the famous 16th-century bridge destroyed 10 November 1993

to the 2003 invasion of Iraq, the United States and its allies had to negotiate and engage with Saddam Hussein's diplomatic representatives in the United Nations. In other cases, some states might not recognize the capacity of other states to conduct international relations precisely because they are considered to be unable to manage their national territories let alone engage with the wider world. Terms such as 'failing states' and 'quasi-states' have been used to imply that some countries in regions such as West and Central Africa can neither claim exclusive control over their territory nor secure internal order. In other words, Western governments frequently represent states such as Somalia and/or the Democratic Republic of Congo as inadequate and, moreover, unable to regulate flows of drugs, money, and arms trafficking. It is important to recall, however, that some of the earliest geopolitical writers such as Kjellen objected to this excessively legalistic conception of sovereignty precisely because it neglected the fact that the geographies of global politics were extremely varied. So terms such as 'failing state' acknowledge in part that the capacities of states vary even if they enjoy similar international recognition to others.

Second, we might consider sovereignty as conditioned by interdependence. In an era of intense globalization, it is unhelpful to presume that states enjoy exclusive control over their territories and accompanying flows with associated levels of mobility. Even the most powerful countries in the world such as the United States and China have had to recognize, in their different ways, that interdependence, while it has not eroded state sovereignty completely, has nonetheless modified politics and policy making. In some areas of social life, such as those encapsulated by national security, countries have attempted to respond to interdependence by enhancing governmental and, in the case of the 27 European Union parties, regional control in the form of immigration control and surveillance while sharing or even conceding formal sovereignty in areas such as human rights protection and economic cooperation. This is sometimes as referred to as 'pooling sovereignty'.

There is universal agreement now that that the characteristic of the modern world is interdependence. But we haven't yet had time to think through its consequences or understood that the international rulebook has been ripped up.

(British Prime Minister Tony Blair, Buenos Aires, 2005)

Third, we might consider sovereignty in purely domestic terms and recognize some states are better able than others to exercise control over their national territories. Comparing the United States with the Democratic Republic of Congo would be stark, as the latter has been consumed by a series of conflicts since the late 1990s, which have led to the death of millions, the mass rape of women and girls, and the destruction of villages. The national government based in Kinshasa does not exercise effective control over its large territory and this emboldened other countries to contribute to instability by funding rival militias. During the cold war, the country previously named Zaire was governed by the plutocratic regime headed by Mobutu (1965–97) and was tolerated by others such as the United States because it was regarded as a vital anti-communist ally in Central Africa. Mobutu was able to maintain some form of domestic sovereignty over the country because he used his well-funded armed forces (supported by exports in minerals and oil) to quell any form of resistance and unrest. This changed after his death in 1997 while in exile in Morocco.

However, even powerful countries such as the United States with well established infrastructures and administrative structures struggle to exercise complete sovereign control. The control of immigration is one such issue, especially with regard to the US–Mexican border, which continues to pose problems for the federal authorities. The US Border Patrol, despite additional investment in personnel, vehicles, and sensory equipment, struggles on a daily basis to regulate the movement of people across the Rio Grande and desert regions of South-Western America. In light of these difficulties, American citizens have created vigilante groups such as the Minuteman Project (http://www.minutemanproject.com/) to patrol and pursue those who are intent on illegally entering the United States. This group, however, is not simply concerned with immigration but voices concerns over the status of Anglophone America and the growing challenge posed by Spanish-speaking communities in the South-West. Little mention is made of the role that these immigrants from the South play in supporting America's agricultural, manufacturing, and service-related sectors. Many of those migrants end up in low-paid jobs with little to no financial and/or personal security.

Fourth, sovereignty is explicitly recognized by other parties in the form of non-intervention. Developed by the Swiss jurist

10. US–Mexican border: children playing soccer along the border fence

Emmerich de Vattel, the idea that states should be able to conduct their own affairs without intervention from outside powers is a vital ingredient of the current political architecture. For states emerging from the shadow of European colonialism, this was particularly significant in facilitating the creation of post-colonial governments. However, American and Soviet administrations frequently interfered in the affairs of other countries, especially those in the so-called Third World, whether in the form of military invasions, economic blockades, cultural penetration, political marginalization, and/or sanctions. For example, the United States invaded the Dominican Republic in 1965 and destabilized Chile in 1973 because it feared the emergence of further socialist governments in the Americas following the successful consolidation of the 1959 Cuban Revolution associated with the leadership of Fidel Castro. The Soviets sent tanks into Budapest in 1956 and again into Prague in 1968 in order to crush reformist governments.

In other areas of international life, many states have actively encouraged the qualification of the principle of non-intervention, as developments in human rights protection would seem to testify. The international community as represented by the United Nations' permanent members has not always responded so readily to evidence of massive human rights violation and genocide in some places such as Darfur (Sudan) despite agitation from pressure groups and other states.

However, in April 1999 bombing by NATO forces of Serbian positions in Kosovo was justified by the protagonists on the basis that they were violating Serbian national sovereignty because the latter was engaged in massacres of the Kosovo-Muslim community. While critics highlighted the lack of United Nations Security Council authorization for this intervention, NATO countries have been accused in other regions of being unwilling to intervene when and where Muslim communities suffered human rights violations and killings. Palestine in the Middle East and the disputed region of Kashmir are frequently remarked upon in this regard. Critics conclude that the principle of non-intervention is more likely to be discarded if the parties suspected of human rights violations and even genocide neither possess substantial military forces (including nuclear or other weapons of mass destruction) nor a network of powerful allies such as the United States as in the case of Israel. In 2005, the UN Summit Outcome Document (particularly Articles 138 and 139) concluded that other states should intervene in exceptional circumstances and that there is a 'responsibility to protect', which places responsibilities on potential interveners and the targets of intervention.

Self-defence? Iran and the acquisition of nuclear weapons

In January 2007, Israeli and British newspapers reported stories that Israel believes that military action against

Iranian nuclear facilities is necessary. Iran, according to this analysis, cannot be allowed to possess a nuclear weapon capability. For a country which is deeply sensitive about how it has been pressurized and/or threatened by outsiders in the past (whether in the form of support for a coup in 1953 or backing Saddam Hussein in the Iran–Iraq war of the 1980s), any talk of violating territorial integrity will further enhance domestic support for exactly such a nuclear programme.

The dominant geographical imagination to be found within Iran is composed of two elements. First, Iran is a regional power with a long history of extraterritorial influence in the Middle East and Central Asia. As with Britain, Iran is also a former imperial power. Second, Iran is a besieged country (and culture) surrounded by Arabic-speaking neighbours and hostile powers such as Israel backed by the United States. Any attempt to engage Iran must, therefore, recognize this context and it is unlikely that military bombing, regime change, and/or further isolation will persuade conservatives in Iran that nuclear weapons acquisition is anything but a shrewd strategic decision.

Some states are better able to exercise effective sovereignty in the sense that they claim a capacity to control and administer their national territories and regulate flows of money, people, goods, ideas, and/or technology. Others possess greater extraterritorial capacities such as the United States and China and are able thus to conduct genuinely globalized relations. This capacity to interfere and engage with other states, other communities, and other regions was of course recognized by some of the earliest geopolitical thinkers. The post-Columbian era, as Halford Mackinder noted, was likely to be characterized by more intense relationships as states recognized that the world was being compressed by new technologies including transportation. Time-space compression has become even more intense and the term globalization has been widely used to encapsulate those shifts in the human experience notwithstanding the arguments over its geographical intensity and significance.

Geopolitical architecture in an age of intense globalization

If we want to understand more fully how global geopolitics has changed since Mackinder's era, then we need to examine how states amongst others have responded, resisted, and regulated processes associated with globalization. If traditional geopolitical thinking was preoccupied with states and the changing fortunes of European empires, then more recent writings have explored the role of non-state actors, networks, regional organizations, transnational corporations, and international governmental organizations. While states and concepts such as sovereignty remain highly significant, a web of interdependence is changing international relations and accompanying global geographies. It is now common to read that states possess permeable borders and that governance is expressed in a more global and polycentric manner, as institutions such as the World Bank, the United Nations, global media corporations, the World Trade Organization play their part in shaping global behaviour.

The notion of intensity is important here because of mounting evidence that states have had to adapt to ever more issues and flows that possess an ability to transcend international boundaries and exclusive sovereignties. The list would undoubtedly include global climate change, human rights, drug trafficking, and the spectre of nuclear annihilation. Over the last 60 years, a particular form of global order was said to have prevailed following the defeat of Japan and Germany in 1945. Sponsored by the victorious United States and its allies including Britain, it has been characterized by three key features – the development of a global capitalist economy, the creation of the United Nations, and the promotion of liberal democracy. The United States was instrumental in creating a new economic order based on the creation of two institutions: the International Monetary Fund (IMF) and the World Bank. These bodies, first considered at Bretton Woods, New Hampshire, in 1944, would aim to establish international economic stability and provide funds for post-war reconstruction.

Bretton Woods: the ending of an international economic order?

The Bretton Woods system of international monetary management was intended to establish the rules governing post-war commercial and financial relations. The spectre of aggressive forms of economic nationalism was to be banished in the process. At the heart of this system were 44 nations who attended the United Nations Monetary and Financial Conference in July 1944. Once it had been ratified in 1946, each country had to accept that the exchange rate of its currency would remain within a fixed value banding so that the International Monetary Fund could help promote and manage global financial stability. In 1971, the system of fixed currencies collapsed and the United States suspended the conversion from dollars to gold.

After 1971, international currencies were no longer tied to particular exchange rates and international financial flows increased. A number of world cities, such as New York, Paris, and London, emerged as major hubs of the post-Bretton Woods era.

Second, the creation of the United Nations in 1945 was instrumental in helping to manage and regulate the behaviour of states in the post-war world.

The United Nations Charter played a key role in establishing sovereignty norms as well as other interventions such as the

11. The United Nations headquarters buildings and most of the flags, taken from across First Ave, during the 60th session of the General Assembly. Framed in marble, the 39-storey office structure is known as the Secretariat building. To the left is a partial view of the General Assembly building

General Agreement of Tariffs and Trade, which sought to promote global free trade. Third, the promotion of liberal democracy by the United States as the preferred system of political expression was critical in legitimating their role in the ensuing cold war struggle involving the Soviet Union and China who publicly promoted socialist revolutions. As a consequence of the collapse of the Soviet Union in 1991 and the decline of socialist regimes in Eastern Europe and elsewhere, institutions associated with the economic and political imprint of the United States have effectively prefigured and advocated the prioritization of global capitalist development based on free trade, open markets, and foreign direct investment. Transnational corporations have facilitated the consolidation of such a global economic landscape through their investment and production activities.

From Yalta to Berlin: the overturning of European political boundaries

In February 1945, the Soviet Union, the United States, and Britain participated in a meeting in the Crimean resort of Yalta. This conference involving Stalin, Roosevelt and Churchill effectively determined the fate of post-1945 Europe. The main outcomes were: the Soviet Union would join the United Nations in return for a buffer zone in Eastern and Central Europe; the Soviets would declare war on Japan; Germany and Austria would be occupied and divided into four sectors and managed by the three conference participants plus France; Germany would have to pay reparations; and countries such as Estonia and Latvia were allowed to remain under Soviet occupation.

It would take another 44 years before the geopolitics of Europe was to be fundamentally altered by the collapse of the East German regime and other communist governments in Eastern and Central Europe. The break up of the Berlin Wall

(built in 1961) was one of the most memorable moments of that transformation. By the end of the 1990s, the Soviet Union had disintegrated, former Eastern European communist governments had joined the European Union (EU) and the North Atlantic Treaty Organization (NATO), and Russia had formed new partnerships with both the EU and NATO.

The ramifications for the state in an era of intense globalization have been much debated. For some, the state has been eclipsed by these intense demands of the global economic and political order. Economic institutions such as the World Bank and IMF are able, especially in sub-Saharan Africa and Asia, to exercise considerable control over government expenditure and macro-economic policy where and when states have requested financial assistance. So-called structural adjustment programmes (SAP) have imposed accompanying conditions, which might include demands that governments cut public expenditure or ease restrictions on foreign investment. During the cold war, such international economic arrangements had geopolitical implications as US-dominated international organizations such as the IMF rendered greater control and influence over regions, such as West Africa, considered to be strategically significant because of their natural oil and natural gas resources. Marxist geographer David Harvey has referred to 'accumulation by dispossession' to highlight the manner in which international institutions have facilitated access to Third World markets and resources. In other regions of the world such as South-East Asia, international loans were directed towards states considered to be allies in the struggle against Soviet and/or Chinese-backed socialist ambitions. Countries such as South Korea and Malaysia were the beneficiaries in this regard, especially during the Vietnam conflict. American administrators in particular feared that if Vietnam fell to communist forces then other neighbouring countries would also be vulnerable to socialist interference.

Other commentators contend that international economic organizations such as the IMF or transnational corporations depend on their relationship with states, albeit one that has been transformed by global flows and networks. States ultimately created the post-war economic and political order and the United States was the most significant in this regard. Moreover, property, taxation, and investment laws both regulate and protect the activities of transnational corporations. The notion of a 'transformed state' is more helpful in the sense that it can be used to highlight in which ways globalization has altered the 'state of affairs' including global political order. As the economic geographer Peter Dicken has opined, states continue to shape specific business and economic activities and regulate within and across their national jurisdictions. Ironically, there are now more states than ever, at a time when some observers have predicted the demise of the state as a direct consequence of intense globalization.

The implications for geopolitics are profound. On the one hand, the ending of the cold war witnessed new states and regional organizations such as Slovenia and the Commonwealth of Independent States (CIS) respectively. The collapse of the Soviet Union and the gradual incorporation of Russia and China into international economic bodies such as the World Trade Organization (WTO) have highlighted how former communist/socialist countries are embedded within the networks and structures associated with global capitalist development. Along with widespread democratization in Eastern Europe, Latin America, and parts of Asia and Africa, policies associated with neo-liberalism such as open markets and foreign direct investment are hegemonic. A deregulated vision of world geography has prevailed – the globe as a border-free zone, which encourages flows of investment and goods. The state was intended to be a facilitator of business and some large US-based companies such as Enron were, at one point, well able to take full advantage of the relative lack of judicial and fiscal structures. During the

1990s, commentators such as Francis Fukuyama lauded the triumph of these ideas and practices associated with US-sponsored neo-liberalism and democracy.

On the other hand, it was also obvious that democracy in the form of free elections and elected representatives was not the norm in all parts of the world including China, sub-Saharan Africa, and parts of the Islamic world. Moreover, even those countries considered by some to be democratic were radically different to Western European and American models. The adoption of economic neo-liberalism has attracted a great deal of opposition in many countries in the Third World as well as Western Europe and the United States. The emergence of an anti-globalization movement is perhaps one of the most obvious manifestations of that resistance to the hegemonic presence of the United States and its advocated forms of neo-liberal global order. This movement, which is incredibly diverse, is often described as 'new' because these bodies appeal to transboundary communities and thus seek to subvert a world based on bounded territories and international frontiers. These groupings frequently do not seek to establish formal political representation in any one country.

The most high-profile anti-globalization demonstrations occurred in cities such as Cologne, Genoa, London, and Seattle. Frequently coinciding with meetings of the WTO or G8, anti-globalization critics are censorious of the way neo-liberalism has eroded national boundaries and thus exposed communities to unwanted interference from global corporations, international institutions, and/or hegemonic powers. At its heart lies the concern that certain kinds of flows are overwhelming local places and communities and that national governments are not able or willing to mitigate those flows as they intersect with territories. Arguably one of the most dramatic examples of anti-globalization endeavour occurred in Seattle in November 1999. Timed to coincide with a WTO meeting, 60,000 people descended on the Pacific Coast city to register their grievances against corporate globalization and compelled the United States to use its military forces in order to restore civic order. The protests continued around the world and in 2001 a World Social Forum was established in Brazil to consolidate and coordinate resistance to these neo-liberal forms of globalization. Over 100,000 people attended Forum meetings in India and Brazil in 2004 and 2005 respectively.

The anti-globalization movement remains diverse and although now partly preoccupied with other anti-war movements in resisting the War on Terror and the occupation of Iraq, its activities have contested and disrupted the existing neo-liberal economic and political order. The protests in Seattle and elsewhere have forced states hosting meetings of the WTO, G8, and World Bank to spend more time and money on security arrangements. However, the post-11 September era has also provided new opportunities for rich states and regional organizations such as the European Union to consolidate their national boundaries and, as the Doha meeting of the WTO demonstrated in November 2001, to negotiate ever harder to place restrictions on agricultural and industrial exports from the Global South.

The United States and a new 'empire'

The response of the United States, following the attacks launched on 11 September 2001, has been much analysed and debated. It is now common to describe that event as a major turning point in the contemporary history of the United States and global order. Sixty years earlier, the United States was instrumental in establishing a political and economic order based on the United Nations, the World Bank, and the International Monetary Fund. Faced by an unprecedented loss of civilian life within continental America, the Bush administration embarked on a War on Terror in close liaison with allies such as Britain, Pakistan, and Australia in the pursuit of those who masterminded the attacks and other flows of terror. The diplomatic and military elements of this mission have linked Afghanistan, Iraq, Iran, the Yemen, Sudan, and Syria. Regional allies such as Israel, Qatar, Saudi Arabia, and Pakistan have been critical in facilitating intelligence sharing and hosting military operations against elements suspected of being part of terror networks intent on causing destruction and mayhem around the world.

President Clinton (1993–2001)	President Bush (2001–2009)
Globalization	**Global War on Terror**
Information power	**Military power**
International law	**Pre-emption**
Multilateralism	**Unilateralism**

The War on Terror is highly significant in geopolitical terms because it has been directed against states accused of harbouring terror groups and associated networks. The main objective of the War on Terror has been to destroy the Al-Qaeda network and its leading personalities, notably Osama bin Laden and his deputy the Egyptian born doctor, al-Zawahiri, both associated with 9/11 and earlier bombings of American Embassies in East Africa. Battle-hardened by their experiences of fighting the Soviet occupying force in Afghanistan, Al-Qaeda was created in the 1980s and funded and armed by American, Pakistani, and Saudi sources. Outraged by America's placement of troops on the Arabian Peninsula during the 1991 Persian Gulf War, the Al-Qaeda network has sought to target American interests around the world and made connections with local insurrections in South-East Asia, South-East Europe, and Russian-occupied Chechnya.

While most governments were swift to express international sympathy for the victims of the 11 September attacks, the manner in which the Bush administration constructed and implemented the War on Terror strategy has attracted considerable opprobrium. For the critics, the assault on Iraq in 2003, the use of indiscriminate torture, and the establishment of camps such as Camp X-Ray and Delta in Cuba point to a worrying lack of regard for international law and convention. While there is an emerging global consensus that these principles should be constrained when confronting overwhelming evidence of genocide and/or human rights violations, the role of international legitimacy is considered crucial for maintaining the prevailing doctrines and geopolitical architecture. The Bush administration's decision to implement a doctrine of pre-emption is of specific concern because it would reserve the right for the United States to take military action against non-state groups and/or states which it perceives as hostile.

Geopolitically, however, the actions of the United States also indicate an increased adoption of extraterritoriality, which threatened to undermine important principles associated with non-interference and national sovereignty. National Security Strategies (2002, 2005) have been clear in this regard; the United States will not wait to be attacked again. Creating garrisons of extraterritoriality such as the ones to be found at the US naval station at Guantanamo Bay in Cuba to circumvent American constitutional protections also gives rise to considerable concern that, as the Italian philosopher Giorgio Agamben has noted, a 'state of exception' becomes the norm in an era characterized as a War on Terror. This means that, in the case of the United States, a state of emergency is used to justify the degradation of the legal status of the individual and thus produce a legally unnamable and unclassifiable being. The men captured in Afghanistan by American forces in November 2001 were neither classified as prisoners of war (under Geneva Conventions) nor accorded the status of people charged with crimes according to American laws.

12. US naval station, Guantanamo Bay, Cuba

The extraordinary rendition of suspected Al-Qaeda prisoners from locations in Central Asia, the Middle East, and elsewhere has implicated a host of other countries including Britain in facilitating and/or supporting a process which seeks not only to isolate individuals geographically and legally from rules and conventions designed to protect prisoners but also to transfer them to a legal and geographical 'state of exception'. If some of this discussion sounds Kafkaesque then perhaps readers might, if they have not already, read the shocking bio-geographical account of a British citizen, Moazzam Begg. In *Enemy Combatant*, he describes how he was extracted from Pakistan then taken to Afghanistan, and finally transported to Camp X-Ray in Cuba. The cells were labelled Somalia, Lebanon, USS Cole, Nairobi, Twin Towers, and Pentagon, as if simply listing the places implicated in terror attacks against US citizens justified the nature of the detention. Questioned by American and British security officials, he struggled to establish his innocence. Labels such as 'illegal combatant' were horribly effective in denying this individual and others an opportunity to establish what charges are being brought and the nature of the evidence that might support such an accusation. Imagine the horror and outrage if an American citizen (or, as some critics have contended, a white British citizen rather than a British Asian) was held by another country and denied access to any due legal process. Some of his fellow inmates were unable to cope with this 'state of exception' and took their own lives and others attempted to do so.

The damage done to the prevailing geopolitical architecture has arguably been considerable. Francis Fukuyama has recently recorded his dissatisfaction with this state of affairs. In a country that was responsible for establishing the United Nations and human rights accords, the abuse of international law, the lack of restraint and the indiscriminate adoption of violence is truly shocking. As Fukuyama records, his support for the neo-conservative intellectuals who have informed Bush's global strategy has drained away as he witnessed the ill-considered assault on Iraq, the failure to appreciate the violent reaction against the United States in the Middle East, the unwillingness to help resolve the Palestine question, and the lack of consideration given to reconstruction in Iraq and Afghanistan after US bombing missions. He finds that doctrines such as pre-emption, regime change, and unilateralism are unlikely to be sustainable in the longer term and are certainly not a replacement for international law, the United Nations, and US-rejected institutions such as the International Criminal Court. The National Security Strategy (2002) is contemptuous of international forums, believing that they are used by weaker states intent on restraining the United States and its global mission to eradicate terror.

The Bush Doctrine based on pre-emption and highly selective multilateralism is the single most important danger confronting the current geopolitical architecture. Moreover, the use by the President of the United States of simplistic reasoning such as 'you are either with us or against us' is having profound geopolitical implications, as some states and regions depending on their compliance are rewarded with financial and military support. Some states in the Horn of Africa and East Africa have been beneficiaries such as Dijbouti, Kenya, and Ethiopia. The prospect of untapped oil reserves in the Gulf of Guinea has also invited additional American interest and led to new investment patterns in West and Central Africa. While the War on Terror provides a geopolitical template, the continent of Africa was described as a major security threat in the National Security Strategy of 2002 because of the high numbers of 'weak' states either unwilling or unable to control flows of people, money, and terror activities. Such a bleak assessment encouraged the Bush administration to establish in 2004 the Pan-Sahel Initiative, which involved Chad, Mali, Mauritania, and Niger in defence cooperation with American forces. It was designed to halt the movement of Islamic militants in the region and $100 million was assigned to the initiative alongside some increases in funding for the so-called Millennium Challenge Account.

While the pursuit of terror networks around the world provides one apparent justification for contemporary American foreign policy, there are also more politico-economic reasons. The world has changed greatly since 1945 and the decision of the Roosevelt administration to help to establish a world order based on the United Nations and a global economy open to American trade and investment. Currently, the US economy is heavily indebted and China is fast emerging as the world's most powerful economy, already attracting the largest amounts of foreign direct investment and the second biggest spender on arms after the United States. China holds $300 billion in US Treasury Bonds and has a vested interest in avoiding an economic conflict with the United States. Both economies have substantial resource needs and it is perhaps unsurprising that American actions in Iraq and the wider region have been interpreted as part of a geopolitical strategy to maximize access to oil and natural gas reserves. America is now heavily dependent on imported oil and has sought to exploit resources held not only in the Middle East but also in Africa, Latin

America, and Central Asia, especially the Caspian Sea region. A recent report by the Council on Foreign Relations (2006) entitled *National Security Consequences of US Oil Dependency* urged the Bush administration to diversify sources and promote energy efficiency and investment in renewable sources.

As China's energy needs are increasing, it is estimated that by 2025 it will require 11 million barrels of oil per day (the current production levels of Russia), an increase of some 6 million barrels per day from 2005. Unsurprisingly, Chinese foreign direct investment has been carefully targeting countries such as Iran, Angola, and Sudan as it seeks to secure additional resources around the world. Unlike the 1970s and 'supply shock', the 2000s have witnessed a form of 'demand shock' as emerging economies such as China are facing rising industrial and domestic demand for power generation and transportation.

Russia and a new era resource geopolitics

In recent months, Russia's state-owned energy corporations such as Gazprom have been exerting greater influence on near neighbours Belarus and Ukraine. Encouraged by high-energy prices and rising demand alongside control of pipeline networks, Russia has used the control of supply to reassert itself. Moreover, it has also pressurized foreign energy companies to accept new strictures over ownership and investment. This apparent bonanza may not last, however, as Russia's energy supplies are expensive to exploit and other major suppliers such as Qatar offer liquefied gas, which is transported via tanker and thus is not dependent on pipeline access.

The European Union, concerned over Russia's reliability as a supplier, produced a new energy strategy (2007), which is intended to diversify energy supplies and promote renewable

sources in the face of external uncertainties. The EU has suggested that it might invest further in liquefied gas terminal facilities so that it can receive greater supplies from Qatar and help develop South American supplies in Bolivia, Peru, and Venezuela.

The scramble for resources, while reminiscent of a scramble for colonial territories in the 19th century, has important implications for the prevailing geopolitical architecture. Some analysts fear that the next generation of wars will be triggered by competition for resource access. The Caspian Sea is frequently described as a potential flashpoint alongside the long-standing extra-regional power interest in the Middle East. While the United States and China have extended their military and financial interests in these regions, Russian geopolitical analysts are alarmed at the build up of this investments in the Caspian, a region still considered part of Russia's 'near abroad'. The Russian government has also been more aggressive in renegotiating pricing and access to natural gas in neighbouring countries such as Ukraine and sought to impose new controls on foreign investment in energy exploration and exploitation within oil-rich regions such as Siberia. It is now common to read within Russian geopolitical circles that the country should use its substantial energy resources to secure a greater global presence. As access to energy resources is likely to become an ever more important determinant of wider global political patterns, territorial competition will intensify. A continued American presence in the Middle East, Africa, and Central Asia will provide further 'grist to the mill' for Islamic militants who resent the presence of American companies and armed forces in the Middle East and wider Islamic world.

At present, America continues to be the dominant force shaping global geopolitics and the War on Terror has provoked substantial increases in military spending and counter-terror investment around the world. In turn, it has triggered further discussion about whether this level of activity is indicative of imperial behaviour. For some neo-conservative commentators such as Max Boot, terms such as 'Empire' have become badges of honour. It is, for some, evidence that the Americans have the right to act imperially (for the greater good) while at the same time securing their national interests. Critics, however, contend that 'imperial America' is engaged in a colonial and racist project designed to subjugate regions and citizens in the Global South for the benefit of political and business elites operating in and beyond the United States.

Scholars remain deeply divided on whether the United States is behaving in an imperial manner. In their best-selling book, *Empire*, Hardt and Negri claim that a farrago of actors including powerful states such as America, firms, and international governmental organizations are working together (not necessarily under any form of hegemonic control) in order to regulate and protect a global market. In their terms, 'Empire' is an apparatus of global rule, which is not tied to one particular territorial centre such as the United States. At present, however, it seems premature to underestimate the continued significance of American political, economic, and military power and its impact in places such as Iraq. In his analysis of America's imperial ambitions, Michael Mann concludes that America does not have imperial power and that a reliance on military solutions is, if anything, a sign of weakness not strength.

As Joseph Nye has said, overwhelming military power is useful for destroying opponents' armed forces and national infrastructure but is less likely to be helpful in resolving conflict and building long-term peace and stability. American cultural and political values have been openly and violently rejected and widespread anti-Americanism in the Middle East and beyond would indicate a decline in what Nye has described as 'soft power'. As he notes:

> Sceptics of soft power ([former] Secretary of State for Defense Donald Rumsfeld professes not even to understand the term) claim

popularity is ephemeral and should not guide foreign policy. The United States, they assert, is strong enough to do as it wishes without the world's approval and should simply accept that others will envy and resent it. The world's only superpower does not need permanent allies; the issues should determine the coalitions, not vice-versa, according to Rumsfeld.

In the longer term, such a hegemonic presence is likely to be conditioned further by the growing presence of China and India and their corresponding resource needs and geopolitical priorities. It is not difficult to imagine that the permanent membership of the Security Council might change as other countries such as India, Brazil, and/or Indonesia demand recognition from those who happened to be on the winning side of the Second World War. However, Japan's quest for a permanent seat at the Security Council is likely to be thwarted by China. The challenge for the United States is to hold on to a legitimacy that has been eroded badly by the Bush administration in its ruthless pursuit of those who carried out the 11 September 2001 attacks. Any short-term advantage, economic or political, from such a strategy is likely to be counteracted by longer term damage to the reputation of America and close partners such as Britain around the world.

Conclusions

The Bush administration's apparent disdain for the existing geopolitical architecture and international law has encouraged expressions of anti-Americanism beyond the Middle East and Islamic world. Moreover, it has also enabled populist governments in Latin America (Chavez in Venezuela and Morales in Bolivia) to play their part in exposing 'American imperialism' and proclaiming an 'an axis of good' at the expense of the United States and its allies. Awash with monies generated by oil and natural gas sales, these South American countries alongside Iran and Russia

13. 'New Phase Blair': the Anglo-Iranian hostage crisis (2007)

have been able to challenge and at times mock the United States, apparently safe in the knowledge that the American economy remains addicted to oil and natural gas supplies. To make matters worse, Iraqi oil production remains underdeveloped because of the continued chaos in the country and a failure to provide a legal framework which would encourage foreign companies to invest and develop wells and infrastructure. Most disturbingly, this current approach to existing international bodies and conventions merely emboldens those Islamic militant critics who can with some evidence point to American disregard for human rights and willingness to bomb, torture, and maim communities in the Middle East and Islamic world. As many critics – both Muslim and non-Muslim – will point out, tremendous cultural damage is done every time American personnel disregard the basic human dignity of others. This is not in any way to diminish the horror perpetuated by Islamic militants, rather it highlights how important it is for the United States to be seen to be operating to the highest national and international legal standards.

The current geopolitical architecture faces considerable challenges as anti-American sentiment sits awkwardly with the activities of anti-globalization movements, Islamic militancy, resource competition, and geopolitical challengers such as China. The United States as the world's largest superpower is also regarded as the champion of neo-liberal forms of globalization. The problem facing administrations after President Bush is how America will not only regain its international legitimacy but also publicly reinvest in international public bodies which helped it to establish a hegemonic presence during the last century. The colonial occupation of Iraq will stand as a marker of American hegemonic ambition and one in which a military presence was instrumental in reshaping Iraq's economic and political infrastructure. In their different ways, Chinese economic power and Islamic militancy have demonstrated that the 21st century, at least according to the Christian calendar, is unlikely to be an unqualified American one.

Chapter 4
Geopolitics and identity

On 12 September 2001, the French newspaper *Le Monde* published a headline, which in effect declared that: We are all Americans now. As an act of solidarity with another country, it was just one of many outpourings of global sympathy following the attacks on the World Trade Center and the Pentagon on the previous day. Prime ministers and presidents quickly contacted President George W. Bush to offer condolences and many of those leaders also had to confront the fact that the crumpled remains of the World Trade Center entombed some of their own citizens. For others caught up in the horror of that day, the British poet W. H. Auden and his poem '1 September 1939' provided some crumbs of comfort:

I sit in one of the dives
On Fifty-second Street
Uncertain and afraid
As the clever hopes expire
Of a low dishonest decade:
Waves of anger and fear
Circulate over the bright
And darkened lands of the earth,
Obsessing our private lives;
The unmentionable odour of death
Offends the September night.

As a consequence of that 'odour of death', 9/11 was immediately understood not only as a tragedy for the United States and the city of New York but also as a global outrage, which took the lives of so many citizens from across the world. The headline emphasized the manner in which questions of identity were geographically and emotionally connected – the local (New York, Pennsylvania, and Washington), the national (United States), and the global. Shortly afterwards, however, the event became reinscribed in overwhelmingly national terms – 'Attack on America'. Tragically, as former Vice President Al Gore has said, the United States has squandered that global goodwill and solidarity by its largely unilateral engagement in Iraq and other activities which have been judged by others to be inimical to international law, such as extraordinary rendition, detention camps, and the doctrine of pre-emption. We are certainly not all Americans now.

It is now, as a consequence, not unusual to read books, articles, and messages on the internet condemning the Bush administration and the United States more generally. For many observers, regardless of their level of familiarity with that country of 300 million inhabitants, the nation is as much associated with sobriquets such as 'the empire of evil' and/or 'rogue state' as it as a 'victim' of terrorist violence. International reputation vexes governments and communities greatly because national identity and an associated set of national purposes matter greatly. Even a country as large and powerful as the United States is concerned with image and identity management. The Dutch political scientist, Peter van Ham, writing in *Foreign Affairs*, contends that questions of image building and representation had become paramount, with a profound shift in the international political paradigm, in what he termed 'a move from the modern world of geopolitics and power to the post-modern world of images and influence':

> these days, individuals, firms, cities, regions, countries and continents all market themselves professionally, often through

> aggressive sales techniques. Indeed, having a bad reputation or none at all is a serious handicap for a state seeking to remain competitive in the international arena. The unbranded state has a difficult time attracting economic and political attention. Image and reputation are thus becoming essential parts of the state's strategic equity.

Political leaders and journalists routinely draw upon geopolitical traditions, visual cultures, and national histories to articulate and consolidate a sense of national identity and/or purpose. Extraordinary moments like the 11 September 2001 attacks (and associated visual images such as the burning edifice of the World Trade Center) should not obscure the more banal forms of nationalism. As Michael Billig has noted, everyday life is replete with practices and symbols indicative of national identities and territories such as flags, currency, 'national news', and references to territory as either the 'fatherland' or in the case of the United States the 'homeland'. Time and space are mobilized by governments to secure national identities – national territories are mapped and special dates are cherished as evidence of national birthdays, such as 4 July in the case of the United States. Some landscapes and sites as opposed to others are judged either to be 'sacred' and/or emblematic of a nation's 'heritage'. Ground Zero in New York stands alongside other places such as the Statue of Liberty as important symbols (both physical and imaginative) of the United States and its self-understandings – as a beacon of liberty and democracy.

As a revolutionary state, like France and Russia, the United States promoted the principles of national self-determination and anti-colonialism but also contributed to the creation of a global order post-1945. During the cold war, that sense of being a model for the wider world to replicate was heightened still further when confronted by a rival national model based on socialism (and, as it turned out, under Stalin the widespread use of imprisonment and terror) as opposed to liberal democracy and capitalism. America's external projection of national identity is only one element, however. At the same time, the United States was championing liberal democracy; African-Americans were struggling to secure their civil rights and participation within that democratic polity. Geographically, African-Americans were excluded from mainstream social and political life and denied opportunities to vote and therefore promote peaceful transformation. Thus any claim to a 'national identity' would need to be scrutinized carefully in the sense of investigating who, what, and where was judged to be indicative of that national identity. A shared sense of history and geography often appears more problematic than political elites care to believe.

This chapter grapples with some of the issues raised by terms such as national identity and argues that an essential element of geopolitical theorizing is preoccupied with this subject. National identity has to be constructed and historians have been at the forefront of noting how national traditions and traits become invented. The making and remaking of national identities is a creative process and also inherently geographical because they are associated with particular places. Identity narratives are not of course restricted simply to the level of the nation state but can and do operate at a variety of geographical scales from the subnational to the pan-regional and finally to the global. Examples to be explored in this chapter include the European Union and other regional organizations and the manner in which other cultural and political groupings such as subnational groupings, social movements, and diaspora challenge particular claims to national identity. As the capacities of states to control their economic, cultural, and political space has been challenged by non-state actors and associated flows, so those claims to exclusive national identities have often become all the more urgent (and potentially dangerous).

Geopolitics and national identity

The creation of the modern international political system based on national states with exclusive territorial jurisdictions is commonly dated to 17th-century Europe. Over the ensuing centuries, national governments emerged and established via diplomacy and international law, a mosaic of states which has now encompassed the earth's surface with the exception of Antarctica and parts of the oceans. As the apparatus of the state began to envelop the everyday affairs of citizens, national governments through their control and/or monitoring of national media and/or school-level education began to concentrate ever-greater energy in the creation and maintenance of a national self-identity.

In the case of Argentina, for instance, which declared independence from the Spanish Empire in 1810, this was considered an essential element in the survival of the nation state. The process of creating what Benedict Anderson has called an 'imagined community' took several forms, one of which was the introduction of so-called 'patriotic education' in the late 19th century to generate a national consciousness. The timing of these educational reforms was not accidental; the government of Buenos Aires had not only extended its sovereign authority over a more extensive geographical territory, including the most southerly region of Patagonia, but also had to contend with new waves of immigrants primarily from Italy and Spain who had to be incorporated and inculcated with a sense of what it was to be an Argentine citizen.

In the regional context of South America, territorial boundaries remained a highly sensitive affair, as countries such as Argentina, Chile, Bolivia, Paraguay, and Brazil negotiated, often with the assistance of nascent national armies, national territories and border regions. This process was largely beneficial for Argentina as it expanded southwards, westwards, and northwards. Others, such as Paraguay, were less fortunate. The so-called War of the Triple Alliance (1864–70) led to a disastrous outcome. Paraguay lost territory and perhaps over 50 per cent of its adult population to a series of wars with Argentina, Brazil, and Uruguay. In the case of land-locked Bolivia, the so-called War of the Pacific involving others such as Chile and Peru led to the loss of a territorial corridor to the Pacific Ocean. While Argentina would be considered a territorial success story by comparison with Bolivia and Paraguay, one event in the 19th century was to have a dramatic impact on subsequent expressions of national identity and purpose – the loss of the Islas Malvinas to the British in 1833.

One of the most important elements of patriotic education was the geographical lesson that Argentina was an incomplete country. Later described as the 'Lost Little Sisters', the annexation of these South-West Atlantic islands continues to grate and remains an integral element in expressions of Argentine national identity. School-level education continues to promote this view and ensures that every young school child can draw an outline of the two main islands (East and West Falkland according to English speakers) at primary level. As the reference to 'Lost Little Sisters' suggests, the territory is often described in highly gendered terms; as a sisterly appendage of the body politic, which is continental Argentina (the Fatherland). It is not surprising, therefore, that when the Falklands were 'invaded' by Argentine forces in 1982, the action was vindicated as an act of geographical salvation after an earlier 'rape' by perfidious Albion. Remarkably for non-Argentine audiences, crowds gathering in the main square proximate to the so-called Pink House cheered the military regime. At the same time, this and other military governments in the recent past were torturing and executing their own citizens. Geographical indoctrination seemed so complete that many in the Republic were willing, at that moment, to celebrate this act of territorial annexation.

The British victory in June 1982 did not resolve this particular territorial crisis. Despite the claims to the contrary by the then Thatcher government, Argentine citizens continue to be informed that this territorial grievance remains outstanding. I recall my first visit to Argentina, on the tenth anniversary of the conflict, and quite how that geographical sensibility endured. If the British were content to commemorate the conflict as something located in

14. 17 June 1982: a Royal Marine of 40 Commando searching an Argentine prisoner at Port Howard on West Falkland, following the surrender of the Argentine armed forces in the Falklands war

the recent past (and at the same time as connected to older British victories such as the Second World War), Argentine media organizations and governments encouraged citizens and indeed visitors to imagine this territorial dispute as ongoing. If you opened a magazine and examined weather reports for the Republic, you would have noticed that the Falklands were labelled as the Malvinas and thus indisputably Argentine. Since the late 1940s, it has been an offence in Argentina to produce any map of the Republic that did not label the Falklands as Argentine and for that matter a portion of the Antarctic closest to the South American mainland. Public maps and murals constantly reminded the citizen and visitor that the islands are geographically proximate to Patagonia. British sovereignty is constantly condemned not only as reminiscent of earlier episodes of imperialism but also indicative of a particularly distasteful form of geographical overstretch. Since 1982, public war monuments in Buenos Aires and elsewhere also provide a further opportunity for geographical and cultural reflection on what should be Argentine national territory.

Islands and national identity: China and Taiwan

Argentina is not the only country to be preoccupied with the recovery of geographically proximate islands. Another example would be China and Taiwan. Japan seized the islands as a colony in 1895 and remained there until their surrender at the end of the Second World War. On losing the Chinese civil war to the Communist Party of China (CPC), the nationalist leader Chiang Kai-Shek fled there in 1949. The Republic of China (ROC) based in Taiwan was judged to be an illegitimate entity by the CPC even if many Western governments considered the ROC to be legitimate. For much of the cold war, one-party authoritarian governments governed Taiwan, while its economic conditioned prospered. As a Western ally, Taiwan enjoyed the protective presence of

the United States. In the 1980s and 1990s, Taiwan embraced a democratic transition and became more assertive in the conduct of its foreign affairs.

The People's Republic of China (PRC) has passed an anti-secession law (2005) decreeing that it will invade if Taiwan ever seeks full independence. Within China, citizens are constantly reminded that Taiwan is an integral part of the PRC and school-level geography plays its part in ensuring that citizens receive proper instruction. Taiwan has frequently been described as a future global flashpoint between China and the United States.

This apparent obsession with the recovery of the Falkland Islands has broader implications for Argentine national identity. On the one hand, it shaped a particular view of the Republic as a geographically violated country, which remains highly sensitive to territorial matters, as immediate neighbours such as Chile would attest. Both countries have argued for much of their histories over their Andean territorial boundary. This has sometimes resulted in seemingly farcical situations in which both sides argue over remote, unpopulated territorial fragments. On the other hand, the annexation of the Falklands in the 19th century allowed later government leaders such as President Perón in the 1940s and 1950s to construct a national vision for Argentina as a country eager to dispense with British and other imperial influence. Moreover, as a leading member of the Non-Aligned Movement, its civilian governments were eager to contain the influence of American and Soviet extraterritorial influence. During the 1960s and 1970s, however, anti-communist military regimes pursued territorial grievances such as the Falklands question and in 1982 hoped and indeed expected that the United States would support their actions. This proved to be a fallacious assumption and American support of the British decision to retake the Falklands was critical in ensuring eventual success.

Argentina's territorial obsessions are not unique and similar stories could be told for other countries such as India and Pakistan, which as a result of partition have had to endure conflicts over northern territories. In all three countries, maps are extremely sensitive in terms of what they depict with regards either to national boundaries and/or territorial ownership. Territorial anxieties also help to shape school curricula and broader self-understandings. The national media in that respect can be extremely significant in not only generating a sense of 'imagined community' but also helping to cement particular self-understandings. As the political theorist William Connolly has noted, 'Identity requires difference in order to be, and it converts difference into otherness in order to secure its own self-certainty'. In Argentina, it is common to read, view, and listen to stories about the disputed ownership of the Falklands and the threat posed by British imperialism. Further visual reminders are provided by seemingly banal objects such as stamps, tea towels, signposts, and badges embossed with the simple claim: the Malvinas are Argentine. In this and other highly territorialized cultures, claims to particular forms of national identity are rooted and resolved by evoking the spectre of British imperialism and American hegemonic power.

While it would be foolish to claim that all Argentine citizens are obsessed with the recovery of the Falklands, there is a widespread feeling nonetheless that this outstanding territorial grievance has an impact on Argentina's standing in the world. Some citizens might judge those who challenge that particular world view not only ideologically suspect but also deserving of harassment and intimidation. I vividly recall having dinner with a leading political scientist Carlos Escudé and his wife in their Buenos Aires flat. As our conversation moved on to the question of the Falklands, he showed me his scrapbook which contained all the death threats he had received in the post. His academic work has been highly influential in critical analyses of Argentine territorial nationalism. This research has not been welcomed by elements of the political right who argue that the recovery of the Falklands is a national priority. By way of contrast, Escudé has shown how this sense of urgency was not always as consistent as some would wish or expect it to be within the Argentine national polity. As an informal adviser to the Argentine Foreign Ministry, he even turned up one day wearing a badge on his lapel that declared the Falklands were British!

The geopolitics of national identity is pronounced in countries such as Argentina because territorial grievances and uncertainties over international boundaries are held to jeopardize claims to national identity. In other countries such as the United States, which have successfully expanded with little direct experience of territorial loss, national identity formation has taken on a different expression. If Argentines worried about their territorial portfolio, Americans have been largely preoccupied with the social and racial character of their national community. The experiences of the Native American, Japanese American, and African-American communities stand in sharp contrast to the experiences of white Protestant Americans, who continue to shape the prevailing political culture of that country. The political geography of the United States has been profoundly shaped by struggles for other minorities to be recognized by the national polity. The civil rights movements of the 1950s and 1960s and the fight to secure civil liberties for African-American communities occurred against the geopolitical backdrop of the cold war. While Rosa Parks and her fellow protestors in Montgomery, Alabama, were struggling to secure her right to occupy a bus seat, the Eisenhower administration was engaged in a titanic struggle with the Soviet Union for the hearts and minds of the world.

If America defined itself by championing liberty and freedom, many African-Americans must have choked on the tragic irony – while American presidents sought to defend freedoms elsewhere, communities inside the United States were being disenfranchised, degraded, and denigrated. So national symbols such as the Statue of Liberty can be interpreted in different ways depending on, for example, community experiences. African-American communities located in cities such as New Orleans, in the aftermath of Hurricane Katrina, made similar politico-geographical connections as it became clear that the Federal Government had been slow to react to the loss of life and property of the poor and the immobile. African-American families were over-represented in both categories.

Another contemporary example, following 9/11, would be the apparently ambivalent role occupied by the Arab-American and the Asian-American communities. Judged by their appearance and skin colour, many Arab-Americans and people of South Asian origin have complained of being subjected to harassment, intimidation, and frequent ejections from scheduled flights because other passengers complained about their demeanour and choice of language – Arabic or Urdu rather than English for instance. As a consequence, the Council of Arab-American Relations has complained that the community feels victimized and stigmatized because of the actions of 19 Saudi and other Arabic-speaking hijackers on 11 September 2001. Far from being inconsequential, this has led to the suggestion that America's War on Terror is leading to new forms of identity politics that prioritize certain expressions of gender, race, and sexuality largely at the expense of ethnic minorities who are now viewed with fear and loathing, especially if they occupy public and confined spaces such as aircrafts, ships, and trains. Even comic-book heroes such as Captain America now battle it out with Islamic terrorists who are depicted as assaulting Christian-American values in imaginary towns such as Centreville.

Identity and territory have frequently enriched one another in the context of nation states. National territories have functioned as seemingly stable platforms for the manufacturing and reproduction of national identities. Institutions such as the national media and education system have and continue to provide the capacity to generate particular representations of national communities as territorially incomplete (Argentina), territorially violated (Palestine), territorially aspirant (Palestine and Kurdistan), and as an example to the wider world (the United States). These self-understandings are not immune from criticism or alternative representations of national identity. In post-1945 Britain, for example, several geographical conceptions of the country and its role in the wider world have been produced and circulated: a world power linked to its nuclear power status and leadership within the Commonwealth, a bridge between the United States and Europe, the special partner of the United States, a regional power located to the north-west of the European continent. We might even understand these as rival geopolitical traditions, which have had significance at different moments of time and space in the last 60 years. In the late 1940s, as a recent victor alongside the United States and the Soviets, many politicians and members of the British public viewed the country as a rightful part of the so-called Big Three. By the 1960s, notwithstanding nuclear weapons and a close relationship with the United States, the American Secretary of State Dean Acheson famously commented that Britain had lost an empire but not yet found a role. Membership of the then European Economic Community (EEC) in 1973 did not resolve this sense of national identity crisis and role in the wider world.

As a child of the 1970s and teenager in the 1980s, I recall a country caught up in a geographical imbroglio based on a special relationship with the United States (personalized by the obvious chemistry between Margaret Thatcher and Ronald Reagan), indifference towards the EEC, and the Commonwealth, which seemed to simply host summits and royal tours. Sustained by routine consumption of James Bond films and other forms of popular culture which seemed preoccupied with Britain's victory over Germany in the 1940s, it was easy for me at least to assume that Britain's role in the world was far larger and more influential than economic or military standing might imply. Having said that, the 1982 Falklands War, while surprising in terms of its outbreak, seemed to coincide with my memories of James Bond saving the world. Now it appeared we were also capable of saving 2,000 people on the far side of the earth's surface. Flippancy aside, these kinds of anecdotal recollections coupled with formal schooling contributes to the geographical imaginations of citizens and connects up to narratives of national identity.

No one with living memory of the Falklands conflict will forget the 'national mood' of Britain, which with exceptions such as sections of the British Labour Party and newspapers like the *Guardian,* represented the British recapture of the Falklands as far more significant than simply a story about a small community located somewhere in the South-West Atlantic Ocean. As Margaret Thatcher noted in July 1982, the 'Great' had been put back into Great Britain. The Falklands had an imaginative importance that far exceeded its modest geographical size, infrastructure, and known resource value and yet just as white Britons might have been taking some comfort in that fact, other communities within the country were highlighting persistent racism, economic marginalization, and the contested condition of Northern Ireland (or as Irish nationalists might contend the Occupied Six Counties). For Argentines, military defeat in June 1982 facilitated the downfall of the military and led the following year to a democratic transition.

Geopolitics and pan-regional identity

National expressions of identity are arguably still the most significant, given the prevailing international political system based on nation states and territorial boundaries. However, identities are not always territorially bounded. Sometimes identities can simply leak beyond particular territorial boundaries or be deliberately produced so that they transcend the existing mosaic of states and their national boundaries. Europe provides one such example and the 1957 Treaty of Rome and its antecedents

15. The stars of the European Union flag

are significant in this regard. Scarred by the experiences of devastating world wars, European political figures particularly in France and Germany, such as Jean Monnet and Konrad Adenauer, were instrumental in initiating a political, economic, social, and cultural process designed to promote European cooperation and eventual integration. For West Germany, recovering from the losses imposed by two global conflicts and territorial partition, the Treaty of Rome was not just about promoting European integration, it was also further evidence that the country sought to reimagine itself as an integral part of a democratic Europe and, as it turned out, a geostrategic ally of the United States.

While the experiences of the Second World War provided the rationale for this project of European integration, the geographical definition of membership was more troubling. Who could join this new economic club? Where did Europe begin and end? Did member countries have to be predominantly Christian in national ethos and outlook? In 1963, Turkey, often described as a geographical bridge between Europe and Asia, first applied to join the EEC and has had a problematic relationship with existing members ever since. Forty years later, Turkey's entry into the European Union remains mired in controversy as some later members such as Austria have articulated fears that this populous country will place considerable economic, political, and cultural strains on the existing membership, and others have drawn attention to the fact that Turkey's commitment to human rights and the protection of ethnic and cultural minorities has been patchy to put it mildly. Lurking beneath debates over labour movement, economic opportunities, human rights, and political integration, critics in Turkey and beyond believe there is a fundamental cultural anxiety concerning the integration of additional Muslims into a Europe that already possesses substantial Muslim communities in France, Germany, and Britain.

Turkey: bridge between East and West?

The notion that Turkey straddles Europe and Asia is common within the popular geopolitical imaginations of states and citizens alike in Europe. However, it is also misleading in the sense that it does not help understanding of the internal complexities of that republic.

Since the creation of modern Turkey, Kemalism has been defined as secular, Western-orientated, and later as anti-communist. The ending of the cold war disrupted part of that national identity and led to resentment that other counties in the former Eastern European bloc were being rapidly integrated into the EU at the expense of a NATO ally to the south-east. However, the very ideals associated with Kemalism have also been responsible for embedding the military in political and constitutional life and the long-term suppression of minorities such as the Kurds. In November 2002, the Islamic-leaning Justice and Development Party won the general election and traditional Kemalists were concerned that the country's commitment to secularism and

Westernization would weaken. Rather than conceive of this development as a weakening of Turkey's traditional claims to self-identity, the AK Party has raised the possibility of developing an Islamic-leaning democracy which might, unlike the experience of Iraq, actually inspire fellow Muslims to pursue similar projects, embracing along the way a commitment to individual rights, democratic norms, and human rights. If accepted within the European Union, Turkey also provides other Europeans with opportunities to reflect on what it means to be European, modern, and Western.

Historically, geographical representations of Europe have changed and it would be fallacious in the extreme to contend that there are secure understandings of this continental space. Recent debates over the future of the European Union have frequently been populated with concerns relating to territory, identity, and sovereignty. In the midst of the Bosnian wars in the early 1990s, European Union states were berated for being weak and failing to intervene in an area proximate to the membership. Bosnian and other European intellectuals poured scorn on the inability of fellow Europeans to come to the aid of a multicultural and multi-ethnic country located only two hours flying time from London and even less from Paris, Bonn, and Rome. The destruction of cities such as Mostar and Sarajevo in 1992 and the massacre of 7,000 men and boys in Srebrenica in 1995 was interpreted by many observers as a damning indictment of this European project to promote values such as integration, tolerance, peace, and democracy.

In the midst of the negotiations relating to a European Constitution, political parties and media outlets debated with some vigour the nature and purpose of the European Union, which now comprised 27 member states. Some political figures on the right wished to see the Constitution embody a 'Christian

16. Istanbul as 'the bridge' between Europe and Asia

European' ethos and place due emphasis on its geographical identity as a distinct civilization. French and Dutch voters later rejected the proposed Constitution and thus effectively derailed the introduction of this particular body of text. For non-Christian observers, the notion that Europe could ever be defined as a Christian space would be alarming, given the long-standing presence of Jewish and Muslim communities throughout the continent and in prospective candidate states such as Turkey. However, it should not be assumed that these cultural-religious questions sit uneasily with secular Enlightenment ideals, as human rights and individual freedoms are attractive to all Europeans including Turks.

One of the greatest challenges facing many European governments including Britain, France, and the Netherlands is the alienation faced by Muslim communities. One of the 11 September hijackers, Mohammed Atta, was deeply disillusioned with German society while studying in Hamburg. In France, rioting in the suburbs of Paris in the summer of 2005 was blamed on the discrimination and racism faced by young Muslim men in particular. Local experiences of alienation coupled with the ongoing crises in Afghanistan, Palestine, Iraq, and Chechnya have contributed to a global sense of grievance. This combination of local, regional, and global religious and geopolitical factors was cited as significant in the motivation of the four men who chose to bomb the London transport system on 7 July 2005.

Such cultural debates over the geographical extent of Europe haunt many narratives of national identity and pan-regional expressions. Turkey's long-standing engagement with the European Union is just one aspect of this predicament, as were the wars that engulfed the former Yugoslavia in the early 1990s. Other areas of pan-European political and cultural life, such as the flow of people both inside the European Union and outside, have frequently provoked anxieties about who is European and who is not. The recent entry of Poland and Slovakia into the EU led some British newspapers to warn that Britain would be 'swamped' as Eastern Europeans migrated to Britain in search of work opportunities. As with immigration from the so-called New Commonwealth in the 1950s and 1960s, some commentators claimed that the country was on the verge of being overwhelmed by people who were not 'like us'. As with contemporary debates over immigration, references to 'swamping' act as a kind of cultural geographical code to enact worries about national and even pan-regional identities. For those with a keener sense of history and geography, countries such as Britain have always been shaped by waves of immigrants and I for one am very happy to be served coffee by the Slovaks, Poles, and Czechs who manage my local café.

The membership of the European Union continues to expand, with Bulgaria and Romania joining in January 2007. While many have been critical of EU institutions and its incapacity to generate an effective sense of purpose and pan-European identity, it is necessary to consider how the EU has encouraged new expressions of national identity. In May 2006, the republic of Montenegro held a referendum for independence and 55 per cent voted in favour of that option at the expense of continued partnership with Serbia. As Luiza Bialasiewicz has noted, the role of the EU is particularly interesting because it established the criteria which the republic of Montenegro should meet in order to have its claims of independence acknowledged. Indeed, the key argument for Montenegrin independence was shaped by a desire to enter the EU, not national independence *per se*. Many Montenegrins were unhappy that their desire to be part of the EU was being effectively suspended because of Serbian unwillingness to surrender suspected war criminals and previous involvement in violent conflicts involving Kosovo and other parts of the former Yugoslavia. The participation of the EU was without precedent and clearly demonstrates how a pan-European organization can play a decisive role in shaping cultural claims to a European identity.

As with the Baltic countries, such as Estonia, Lithuania and Latvia, membership of the European Union was seen as an important part of a transformative process which would allow these states to reimagine themselves as 'European' and at the same time less bound up with the affairs and interests of the former Soviet Union. In doing so, the European Union becomes less geographically defined by Western European states and therefore more internally differentiated.

The identity narratives and political practices associated with the European Union have both complemented and challenged those associated with national states. For some the European Union should be considered as a 'Europe of nations', while others seek to encourage a 'United States of Europe'. One way of dealing with these competing geopolitical visions is simply to resolve them geographically; the Euro-zone and the Schengen Agreement provide examples where some states are members and others are not. The accompanying debates over the geographical extension of Europe are important, as the EU has shown itself willing to extend European Union activities beyond the boundaries of the current membership. In 2006, the EU approved the deployment of a contingent of over 7,000 largely European troops, led by Italy and France, to southern Lebanon. The new UNIFIL force was an unprecedented effort – both in terms of scope but also because it created a new UN–EU peace-keeping force. The EU now contributes to a variety of other humanitarian missions around the world: from the Congo to East Timor to Transdniestria/ Moldova. What is more, both Lebanese and Israeli commentators have called for further European involvement in a territorial region which in the case of Israel is part of European football and singing related contests. The EU has acknowledged Hezbollah is an important non-state organization that needs to be brought into the negotiating equation.

Geopolitics and subnational identity

If regional expressions of identity and purpose complicate the relationship between political entities and expressions of national identity, subnational groupings seeking independence or greater autonomy from a central authority also question any simple assumptions that identities are territorially bounded. Countries such as Japan and Iceland, which are virtually ethnically homogeneous have had less experience of subnational groupings challenging territorial legitimacy and associated claims to national identity. Within Europe, communities such as the Catalan community in Spain and the Walloons in Belgium continue to provide reminders that expressions of national unity and purpose are circumscribed and sometimes violently contested by other groupings that resent claims to a national identity or vision. Nation building is a dynamic process and states such as Spain have alternated between trying to repress and to accommodate competing demands for particular territorial units and representations of identity therein. Over the last 40 years, Spanish governments based in Madrid have granted further autonomy to the Catalan and Basque communities, at the same time as military officials have been quoted as noting that the country would never allow those regions to break away from Spain.

This apparent determination to hold on to those territories has in part provoked groups such as ETA (Basque Homeland and Freedom in English) to pursue terror campaigns that have in the past included bombings and attacks on people and property in the Basque region and major cities such as Madrid. Created in July 1959, it sought to promote Basque nationalism alongside an anti-colonial message which called for the removal of Spain's occupation. The Spanish leader General Franco was a fierce opponent and used paramilitary groups to attempt to crush ETA. This proved unsuccessful and ETA continued to operate after his death in 1975, notwithstanding various attempts to secure a ceasefire in the 1990s. Most importantly, the group was initially blamed for the Madrid bombing on 11 March 2004, which cost the lives of nearly 200 people. The then People's Party government led by Prime Minister Jose Aznar, who had approved the deployment of Spanish troops to Iraq, was heavily defeated at the national election three days later. Islamic militant groups rather than ETA were the perpetrators of the Madrid bombings (called '11-M' in Spain). Interestingly, a national government haunted by low popularity attempted to blame an organization operating within Spain for a bombing that many believed to be a direct consequence of Spain's willingness to support the War on Terror.

While the challenge to the Spanish state posed by subregional nationalisms remains, the use of terror probably receded as a consequence of the March 2004 attacks on Madrid. As with other regional movements, found in Catalonia and Galicia, groups such as ETA play a part in mobilizing narratives of identity which run counter to national stories about Spain and Spanish identities. The separatists unsurprisingly either target property and symbols emblematic of the Spanish state and its 'colonial occupation' or vigorously promote practices and expressions of difference such as languages, regional flags, and maps and in the case of ETA a geographical space that defines and defends the Basque homeland – Euskalherria. It is, however, important to note that not all Basque separatists have supported the activities of ETA in the past.

National rivalries: football and Spain

An insight into the contested national condition is provided by football. The Spanish league (*La Liga*) provides opportunities for fans and political leaders to project their frustrations and ambitions onto the backs of rival football teams. Basque and Catalan teams such as (Athletic Bilbao and Barcelona respectively) are important expressions of regional identity and pride. Matches against Real Madrid (supported by the Spanish dictator Franco) are particularly intense and represent a very real expression of popular geopolitics. Franco attempted to use Real Madrid's success in the European Cup to suppress regional and linguistic differences within Spain. The Catalan language was banned under his period of rule (1939–75).

The apparent challenge posed by subnational groupings is not unique to Europe, however. In China, for instance, the central authorities in Beijing have identified separatist movements in western China as a major security threat, especially post-9/11. Since coming to power in 1949, the Chinese Communist Party has been anxious to preserve territorial integrity in the face of the *de facto* secession of Taiwan and the troubling occupation of Tibet. More recently, Muslim separatists in the far west of China have been represented as a threat to Chinese unity and sense of national identity. In the last five years, the central government has adopted a fourfold strategy to promote national unity – economic investment directed towards those regions containing separatists in the hope of removing grievances over regional inequalities, population movement from East to West China, coupled with an enhanced security presence both internally and via foreign policy decisions such as the pursuing of close cooperation with Central Asian states and Russia. As others have noted, China has used America's War on Terror opportunistically to repress further any communities and groupings judged to be threatening to national security.

For both national states and regional separatists, the struggles to demarcate ownership of territory are considered to be an essential element in enabling particular narratives of identity to be sustained. On the one hand, these struggles in diverse places such as Spain, China, Sri Lanka, or Indonesia help national governments not only to legitimate military and security operations but frequently they also provoke greater levels of financial and emotional investment in narratives of national identity as manifested in popular cultural outlets such as television, schools, and newspapers. The designation of something as a security threat, as Barry Buzan and other scholars of geopolitics and international relations have noted, is often an essential moment in the justification of coercive means as the state is judged to be imperilled. On the other hand, separatist struggles remind us that such claims to national identities are never given. The contemporary condition of Iraq provides a chilling reminder of how colonial borders and multiple identities coexist uneasily and the imposition of infrastructure and national symbols such as a new Iraqi flag is barely adequate when there is little local legitimacy and recognition.

Following 9/11 and the decision by the United States to declare a War on Terror, it is striking how apparent allies such as Russia, China, and others such as Israel have sought to rebrand local separatist/self-determination struggles as part of a broader global narrative of counter-terror. Often geopolitically opportunistic in the extreme, it does highlight the continued importance of geographical scale in political and cultural life. The subnational, the national, and the global are implicated with one another. President Putin, as part of this global counter-terror movement, has represented Russia's violent interventions in Chechnya, which predate 9/11, as a response to the threat facing the territorial integrity of Russia. Ironically, and in large measure because of the disproportionate levels of civilian losses, Islamic militants have seized upon the behaviour of Russian troops to justify not only terror acts in the region, such as the murderous assault on a school in Beslan in neighbouring North Ossetia, but elsewhere in Iraq and Israel.

Geopolitics and civilizations

In 1993, the American scholar Samuel Huntington created something of a stir when he published an essay entitled 'The Clash of Civilizations' in the journal *Foreign Affairs*. As with Francis Fukuyama's contribution 'The End of History', a striking title and opportune timing ensured that the essay received considerable publicity both in the United States and elsewhere, including the Middle East and Islamic world. The article begins in dramatic fashion:

> World politics is entering a new phase, and intellectuals [such as himself] have not hesitated to proliferate visions of what it will be – the end of history, the return of traditional rivalries between nation-states, and the decline of the nation-state from the conflicting pulls of tribalism and globalism, among others. Yet they all miss a crucial, indeed a central, aspect of what global politics is likely to be in the coming years. . . . The clash of civilizations will dominate global politics. The fault lines between civilizations will be the battle lines of the future.

Over the pages that follow, Huntington sets out his intellectual stall with a bold, sweeping analysis of the geographies of global politics rather reminiscent of earliest geopolitical writers commentating at the start of the 20th century.

Critically, Huntington sketches a new world map populated by seven or possibly eight civilizations, rather than one dominated by a geographical heartland. In Huntington's geopolitical world, the principal threat facing Western civilization is judged to be Islam and its associated territorial presence in the Middle East, North Africa, Central Asia, and Asia. While his understanding of civilization is vague, his depiction of Islamic civilizations as threatening is informed by the published writings of the Middle Eastern and Islamic scholar Bernard Lewis. The latter has been instrumental in informing neo-conservative opinion in the United States and more than any other scholar has arguably helped to inform the intellectual framework of the George W. Bush administration with regard to foreign policy options for the Middle East. Unsurprisingly, other well known scholars such as the Palestinian-American academic Edward Said have been scathing of the work of Huntington and Lewis.

In defining Islamic civilizations as inherently threatening to the United States and the West more generally, an identity politics reminiscent of the cold war continues albeit under a different cultural-geographical guise. If communism and the Soviet Union were considered global threats for 60 years, Said and others contend that it is now the turn of Islam and regions such as the Middle East and North Africa to be depicted as dangerous and threatening. Even if such an apparent master-narrative seems simplistic, Huntington's mental mapping of the world contains some extraordinary silences or omissions. For one thing, the notion that the West is defined as Christian seems to neglect the long-term presence of other faith communities in Europe and North America. Moreover, it is difficult to imagine any civilization that has not been influenced by a whole range of flows including people and their faiths and other socio-cultural practices, including language, food, and architecture. Any visitor to Spain and Portugal would be hard pushed not to notice the continued influence of Islamic architecture and the role of Arabic in determining place names, for example.

More worryingly for Edward Said, in an article entitled 'The Clash of Ignorance' and published in October 2001, the idea of a 'clash of civilizations' informs an American world view, which might interpret the attacks of 11 September 2001 in distinctly cultural terms. While some Islamic militants might invoke such cultural terms, the inherent danger in such simplistic labelling of places is that interdependence and complexity are sacrificed in favour of monochromatic simplicities. Again, in Bush's America, there is no shortage of right-wing commentators such as Ann Coulter only too eager to link Christian/Western superiority to a form of American foreign policy which would advocate the unqualified defence of Israel and the destruction of the Islamic world. For the more extreme elements of the Christian evangelical community, the Second Coming of Christ will only be secured once the world encounters Armageddon even via a clash with Islamic militants, or more prosaically via global climate change.

Regardless of the source of global destruction, the 'clash of civilizations' debate has highlighted how narratives of identity are also articulated at a global level. These kinds of debates, however, often neglect key elements such as the historical geographies of colonialism. If one wants to understand the ways in which different places and faiths have interacted with one another then the legacies of cultural, political, and economic dominance and resistance have to be appreciated. Again the inherent danger of the Huntington thesis is that other places and faith communities are simply represented as threatening. Even if they were, it is striking that commentators such as Huntington and Lewis are unwilling to consider in more detail how the experiences of British and French colonial domination in the Middle East shaped and continue to shape contemporary geopolitical relations. Claims to British or French moral superiority were frequently exposed when those countries subsequently bombed, gassed, and massacred the very populations they sought to order and control.

Egypt in the early 1920s and 1930s was filled with foreign soldiers and social spaces were segregated in favour of Europeans in a manner later to be replicated in apartheid South Africa. A mounting sense of humiliation and iniquity in Egypt later played a key role in informing the creation of the Muslim Brotherhood and the anti-colonial campaign against the British thereafter. Egyptian radicals such as Sayyid Qutb later visited the United States in 1948 and reported his dislike of its materialistic culture and racial discrimination, especially against the African-American community. While there have been a variety of sources and contexts which have inspired contemporary Islamic militancy, the living memories of colonial occupation combined with a dislike of the racist nature of Western liberal-democratic states is part of that complex equation. Western powers, with the help of proxy regimes such as Egypt, Saudi Arabia, and Jordan, continued to interfere in the affairs of these states even when they had obtained formal independence. Iranians to this day still highlight the role of the American Central Intelligence Agency in sponsoring a coup against the reforming Mossadegh government in 1953.

The 'clash of civilizations' promises cultural and geographical simplicities which frankly don't square with the complexities of a world filled with interconnected communities. In an age apparently characterized by extremes, such simplicities might make for comforting reading/listening in some parts of the United States or the Islamic world. In the American hinterland, such simplicities might offer comfort to those non-travelling citizens eager to make sense of the profoundly shocking events associated with 11 September 2001. Moreover, it might also provide a kind of geopolitical nourishment to a world view which imagines the United States to be hated because it is so successful. In other parts of the world, the notion of clash might be embraced because it helps to make sense of a world that for many Muslims is characterized by fear, uncertainty, and humiliation on a daily basis. For Palestinians, the daily routine of roadblocks and identification checks is a constant reminder that one religious/national community (often associated with the dominant West) is able to determine the lives of millions.

Against this geopolitical backdrop, bin Laden and his associates present their struggle as one directed against 'Jews and Crusaders' operating in the Middle East and elsewhere. In his publicized speeches, bin Laden has utilized the 'clash of civilizations' to help explain and legitimate the campaign against the United States and its allies including the apostate regimes of Egypt, Jordan, and Saudi Arabia. His desire to create a new Islamic community (umma) is based on the cultural-religious purification of the Middle East and Islamic world. The ejection of Israelis, apostates, and American forces from the region is judged to be critical in achieving this objective. The latter is most clearly articulated in his 'Declaration of a Jihad against the America's occupying the land of the two holy places' and reiterated again in the aftermath of the 11 September 2001 attacks on New York and Washington. It is also perhaps not surprising that the two most formative influences on bin Laden's intellectual world view were the Palestinian Abdullah

17. Colonial Cairo provided the educational and political backdrop to the life and works of Sayyid Qutb

Azzam and the brother of the Egyptian activist and founder of the Muslim Brotherhood, Sayyid Qutb.

As the political geographer John Agnew has recorded by way of a concluding summary on the geopolitical imagination of bin Laden and the Al-Qaeda network:

> The United States is a geopolitical abstraction seen as an earthly Satan. The religious inspiration is fundamental to its [i.e. Al-Qaeda's] goals and to its language. These are a mirror image of the idea of the 'clash of civilizations' proposed by the American political scientist Samuel Huntington in 1993 . . . In this case an Islamic world is seen as in a death struggle with an infidel civilization represented by the United States, captain of the materialist West. . . . Only by expelling the West can the pollution be swept away.

Conclusions

This chapter has been concerned with the role of identity politics in shaping geopolitical relationships. This concern for narratives of identity has been provoked by a desire to further shift our interest in geopolitics away from fixed geographical conditions and the activities of great powers such as the contemporary United States and China. Recent scholarship has focused attention on how a state's relative location is constructed and what strategic meaning is given to its territory. This implies that territory is not inherently strategic, rather it has to be invested with significance. Geopolitical reasoning plays a critical role in assigning values to some communities and territories often at the expense of others. These kinds of activities become all the more poignant when a country is seeking some form of territorial redress or is presumed to be facing some kind of threat from other state and non-state organizations. Within contemporary countries and regions such as Israel/Palestine, Argentina/Chile, and Pakistan/India, there is no shortage of evidence of how forms of geopolitical reasoning are used to secure particular claims to territory and identity. This in turn leads to the frequent justification of military force (either actual or threatened), accompanied by politico-military doctrines of pre-emption and unilateral action. These claims are not only produced within government circles but are frequently reproduced within popular cultural arenas such as newspapers, magazines, and cartoons.

In other cases, comparatively new states such as Estonia and non-state organizations continue to project their own identity narratives. In the case of Estonia, membership of the European Union and the North Atlantic Treaty Organization were significant in reorientating the country away from its association with the Soviet Union and the Eastern bloc more generally. For supporters of this geopolitical transformation, Estonia's cultural future is believed to belong to Europe, which is frequently contrasted unfavourably with non-European Russia. The European Union is conceived of both as an opportunity for Estonia to strengthen its European credentials and also as a safeguard against possible Russian interference. As with West Germany in the 1950s, integration is perceived to be strengthening rather than weakening national sovereignty. The Russian-speaking minority in Estonia are perhaps more cautious about this transformation. Paradoxically, it is 'Europe' that has come to the 'salvation' of that Russian minority (just as it would for minorities in Turkey for instance) because it is axiomatic of European Union membership that laws excluding citizens are either repealed or softened so that minority rights are recognized and protected by both national and European law.

More broadly, this discussion further reiterates the fundamental importance of territory and geographical relationships within global geopolitics. On the one hand, state territories remain terrifically important in defining national identities and it would be a complete exaggeration to claim that globalization has eroded this connection. On the other hand, the state and associated national territory coexist with a host of other geographical connections, which might be described as subnational or regional, let alone at the level of civilization. As a consequence of these permutations, individuals and communities are far more likely to lay claim to multiple identities that cross over national boundaries and identities.

Chapter 5
Maps and geopolitics

Introduction

At times of war and international discord, it is perhaps not surprising that public interest in maps and the places that they represent is greatest. When national survival is apparently at stake, this is understandable and enables national governments to explain and justify the dangers and threats facing citizens. In the aftermath of the Japanese attack on Pearl Harbor, President Roosevelt asked all American citizens to purchase maps and globes so that they could better understand the national security challenges confronting the United States and other allies such as Britain from the threat posed by Germany, Japan, and Italy.

President Roosevelt's 23 February 1942 radio address

We must all understand and face the hard fact that our job now is to fight at distances, which extend all the way around the globe.

Look at your map. Look at the vast area of China, with its millions of fighting men. Look at the vast area of Russia, with its powerful armies and proven military might. Look at the British Isles, Australia, New Zealand, the Dutch Indies, India, the Near East, and the continent of Africa, with their

resources of raw materials, and of peoples determined to resist Axis domination. Look too at North America, Central America, and South America . . . I ask you to look at your maps again, particularly at that portion of the Pacific Ocean lying west of Hawaii. Before this war even started, the Philippine Islands were already surrounded on three sides by Japanese power. On the west, the China side, the Japanese were in possession of the coast of China and the coast of Indo-China, which had been yielded to them by the Vichy French. On the north are the islands of Japan themselves, reaching down almost to northern Luzon. On the east are the Mandated Islands – which Japan had occupied exclusively, and had fortified in absolute violation of her written word.

The islands that lie between Hawaii and the Philippines . . . these islands, hundreds of them, appear only as small dots on most maps. But they cover a large strategic area. Guam lies in the middle of them – a lone outpost which we have never fortified.

The United States public responded to this presidential urging and purchased maps with considerable gusto, much to the commercial advantage of cartographic publishers such as Rand McNally. The National Geographical Society and its famous magazine *National Geographic* also enjoyed a wider readership. By the time American troops entered into military action in Europe, Asia, and the Pacific, citizens wanted to know where places such as Guadalcanal and Normandy were located on the global map. This quest for geographical certainty became all the more poignant when relatives were informed that family members were not going to be returning alive from those scattered theatres of war.

War, maps, and geography form a powerful triumvirate with one another. Accurate geographical information is vital as military

18. FDR and the 'fireside chat'

commanders and political leaders consider lines of supply, topographic advantage, modes of advancement, and possible retreat. The new maps which emerged in the 1940s showed American citizens the scale and extent of military operations across three continents as well as emphasizing a new polar-centred projection. As a consequence, readers and viewers were reminded of something rather significant – the United States may well be surrounded by two substantial bodies of water (the Atlantic and Pacific Ocean) but it was also at its northern edges proximate to the Soviet Union and northern Europe. While the full extent of this shift towards the North Pole was not fully felt until the onset of the cold war and the rise of the Soviet Union as a geopolitical threat, it did help to cognitively reposition the United States. Arguably, these kinds of cartographic shifts contributed to a new kind of geographical consciousness, which resurrected a more internationally orientated country eager to shape the post-war global order.

This chapter explores five cartographic moments for the purpose of further elucidating the connections between geopolitics and maps. First, the maps produced by Halford Mackinder are revisited because they present one of the most startling attempts to represent and interpret a new global order at the start of the 20th century. Later maps and writings by other geographers such as Isaiah Bowman played a significant role in reshaping the international boundaries of Europe, following the end of the First World War. These maps possess a long cultural afterlife as even today they are discussed and digested by Americans, Russians, and other political commentators and journalists in Latin America, Iran, and China. The reasons for this renaissance of interest vary depending on the location of readers. For instance, Uzbek security intellectuals have taken an interest because Mackinder described Central Asia as the 'geographical pivot of history'. American strategists and historians such as Paul Kennedy have eagerly returned to these maps in order to understand better why America is interested in Central Asia and the Middle East – resource access and territorial advantage loom large in their accounts.

Second, Isaiah Bowman's role on the Inquiry Committee and contribution to the 1919 Peace Conference is considered. As Europe entered an inter-war period, new political and ethnic boundaries were imposed on a changing continental map. Bowman played a major part in ensuring that political and cartographic transformation, which arguably continues to have a profound impact today on Europe and proximate regions such as the Middle East. Two empires – the Austro-Hungarian and the Ottoman – had disintegrated and the peace-makers based at Paris confronted the prospect of further instability and even revolution in places such as Bulgaria and Romania. Territory was believed to be an instrument of peace and good boundaries were therefore essential in the promotion of order and stability. Redesigning Europe, informed by principles such as self-determination (that an identifiable population had the right to choose the state it belongs to), proved to be a great deal more complicated than simply changing the lines on a map. The British creation of Iraq in the early 1920s was only one such cartographic creation that currently haunts American-sponsored attempts to manufacture a functional and stable democracy.

Third, Frank Capra's *Why We Fight* series is investigated, with particular attention given to *The Nazi Strike,* because it brought the maps and geographical vocabularies associated with Halford Mackinder to a wider public domain. Produced for the United States War Department and the Signal Corp, the series was immensely important in explaining to viewers the political and geographical reasons behind the decision of the country to declare war on Germany and Japan. The series was hugely popular in the United States and presented a straightforward perspective on population, resources, and geographical location, which centred on the intrinsic power of the Euro-Asian heartland. Alongside new maps being popularized in newspapers and magazines, the geographical imagination of American citizens was being radically reshaped by war. This was to be profoundly important in subsequently preparing the imaginative terrain for a new global confrontation – the cold war.

Fourth, the emergence of new polar-centred maps is reviewed not least because it emphasized the lack of geographical distance between the two superpowers during the cold war. The invention of the long-range strategic bomber coupled with the inter-continental ballistic missile development played a critical role in this regard as time and space appeared to be annihilated. People spoke of world distances in terms of hours and minutes rather than weeks and days. Both sides invested in the collection, assessment, and dissemination of maps and photographs of other places. Spy flights, submarine surveying, and satellite photography were essential elements in this endeavour. Most famously, in October 1962, photographs taken by an American U2 spy plane performed an essential role in informing the Kennedy administration's decision to confront the Soviets over their decision to locate missile facilities in Cuba. A Third World War was averted when the Soviets agreed to remove those missiles and President Kennedy resisted pressure from his military personnel to launch nuclear strikes against the Soviets.

Finally, we contemplate one recent endeavour by the American strategist Thomas Barnett to produce a new global map in the aftermath of 9/11 and the subsequent War on Terror. Published in the magazine *Esquire* in March 2003, on the eve of the US–UK invasion of Iraq, his map dividing the world into a core and gap attracted much media and academic attention. For detractors, the map became a leitmotif of the Bush administration's simplistic political mappings of the world. For supporters, Barnett's map alongside the commentary captured the failings of many countries and regions, which appeared to be insufficiently connected to the global economy. As a consequence of their disconnection, they were judged to be more likely to be susceptible to hosting illegal arms trafficking, terror networks, and criminal activity.

Despite the occasional claim to the contrary, maps as images of political space are never neutral or transparent representations of reality. Writing in the midst of American bombing raids (which depended on cartographic intelligence) during the Vietnam conflict, the French political geographer, Yves Lacoste asserted:

> The map, perhaps the central referent of geography, is, and has been, fundamentally an instrument of power. A map is an abstraction from concrete reality, which was designed and motivated by practical (political and military) concerns; it is a way of representing space, which facilitates its domination and control. To map . . . serves the practical interests of the State machine.

They are, as many critical cartographic studies by writers such as Brian Harley and Denis Wood have demonstrated, reflections of knowledge and power even if they can also be beautiful and transfixing. Geographers and cartographers have frequently been employed by government agencies including the military to produce maps for their political leaders, whether it is the Survey of India, the Falklands Islands Dependencies Survey, US Army Corp of Engineers, or the Soviet Military Topographic Service. Maps have also played an important role in the history of particular countries such as inter-war Germany where cartographers played a major role in raising public consciousness about a 'Greater Germany' and the territorial injustices caused by the 1919 Peace Conference.

The geographical pivot of history: Halford Mackinder and the post-Columbian era

Halford Mackinder remains one of the foremost figures in British geography and even to this day Oxford University continues to appoint a Mackinder Chair in Geography. Appointed a fellow of the Royal Geographical Society in his early twenties, Mackinder was appointed as a Reader in Geography at Oxford and later became director of the London School of Economics. He was elected a Member of Parliament and became a prominent supporter of Joseph Chamberlain and the imperial reform movement. Like many of his contemporaries in politics and academia, he was preoccupied with the growing presence of Germany and the United States in global economic and political affairs. Geography, he contended, was an essential element in the education of British citizenry because, as he noted in 1907,

> our aim must be to make our whole people think Imperially – think that is to say in spaces that are world wide – and to this end our geographical teaching should be directed.

He later became a member of the Colonial Office's Visual Instruction Committee (COVIC) and played a major role in shaping future educational materials for schools and the wider reading public alike.

In January 1904, Halford Mackinder presented his paper 'The Geographical Pivot of History' to the Royal Geographical Society in London. Illustrated with several maps, it offered a sweeping analysis of global history and geography. His talk coincided with a period often characterized as an era of global time/space compression. Between 1880 and 1914, the historian Stephen Kern has noted the world was profoundly changed by the imposition of standardized time, the invention of the radio, the consolidation of the railways, the introduction of flight coupled with the culmination of a European colonial project initiated by Spain in the 15th century. In Mackinder's judgement, the world was about to enter a post-Columbian era where there would be little opportunity for imperial states such as Britain to make new territorial conquests because there were few opportunities left to pursue.

The polar regions aside, Mackinder's presentation combined history, geography, and politics in order to promote a way of seeing the world as a whole. The timing of the talk was significant and echoed an emerging pan-European geographical orthodoxy. As Mike Heffernan has noted, French policy makers and journalists were also preoccupied with the subject and the French newspaper *L'Illustration* published an essay in 1900 about the changing global geopolitical scene alongside a series of maps depicting the inevitability of large-scale continental states. On the other side of the Atlantic, the decision of Theodore Roosevelt's administration to expand America's portfolio in Cuba, Puerto Rico, Guam, and the Philippines marked a new phase of imperial expansion by the United States. Public interest in maps and pictorial representations of Cuba and the Philippines expanded, as American citizens were eager to locate these possessions on newly updated maps, charts, and globes. The American Geographical Society (established in 1854) and the more popular National Geographical Society (created in 1888) played their part in stimulating the geographical imagination of members and subscribers to the *National Geographic*. So just when Mackinder warned that his compatriots needed to appreciate the global stage more than ever, American citizens also sought to expand their geographical horizons.

In the post-Columbian era, Mackinder contended that countries such as Britain would have to achieve relative efficiency gains rather than pin their hopes on acquiring new territories. However, as the balance of power that had previously favoured sea powers such as Britain was coming to a close and increasingly shifted towards supposedly land-based powers such as Germany and Russia, the invention of the railways was held to be catalystic. Mackinder believed that an area of the world called by him the 'Heartland' held the key to the future distribution of power and resources. This equated to a vast portion of the Euro-Asian landmass and contained great resource and demographic potential. As Mackinder noted,

> The oversetting of the balance of power in favour of the pivot state . . . would permit of the use of vast continental resources for fleet-building, and the empire would then be in sight. This might happen if Germany were to ally herself with Russia.

Whoever controlled the Heartland, Mackinder contended, had the potential to dominate the entire world. If Britain was not wary then a Russo-German consortium might enjoy such global hegemony because they would have the resources to mobilize and project land- and sea-based power.

In order to achieve domination, the 'pivot area' was considered to be the entry/exit to this Heartland. In his sweeping analysis of world history, Mackinder noted a recurring geographical pattern – successive imperial entities had fought for control of this region, which would now be equated with modern-day Siberia and Central Asia. Writing in 1904, Mackinder was only too well aware that the British had been locked into a so-called 'Great Game' with the Russians for control over this 'pivot' because it was proximate

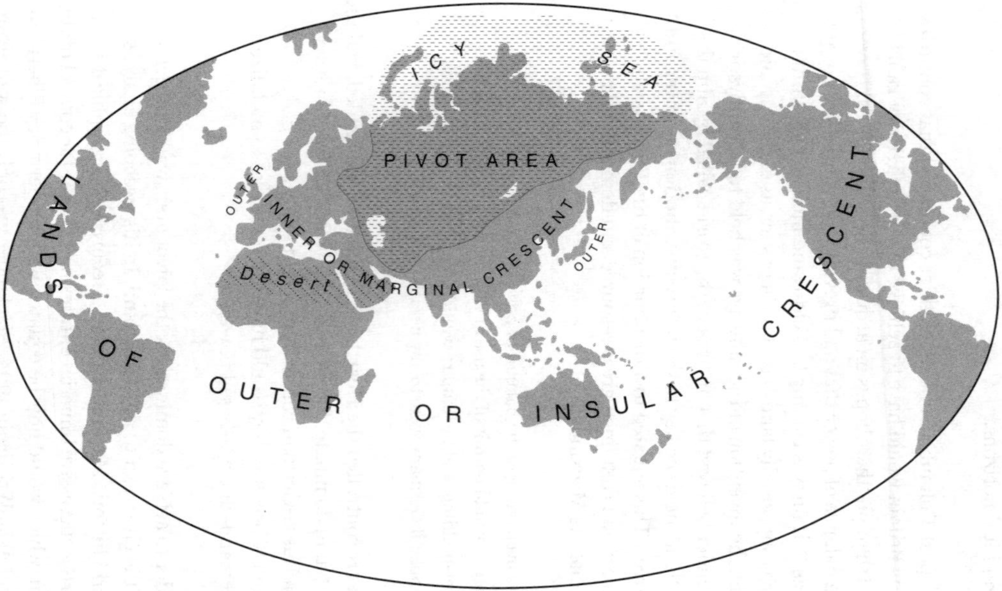

19. The geographical pivot of history

to British India. Maps and surveys played their part in this Anglo-Russian encounter, as both sides were eager to develop geographical intelligence in order to promote their territorial and resource interests.

Accompanying his analysis of this 'geographical pivot' and future great power struggle was a map, which has been understood as one of the most important ever to be produced by a professional geographer.

Using a Mercator projection, the map enlarges Russia and Greenland and radically shrinks Africa and Latin America. The viewer's attention is immediately drawn to the centre of the map and in this case the portion of the globe labelled as the pivot area. Other swathes of the Earth are depicted as the inner or marginal crescent, the outer or insular crescent and North Africa and the Arabian Peninsula are merely described as desert. Antarctica does not feature on the map at all.

While Mackinder's cartographic and intellectual influence on British foreign policy making has been much debated, his global vision was greatly appreciated by a subsequent generation of German scholars anxious to understand the machinations of power. While he overestimated the strategic significance of the Russian 'heartland' and underestimated the emerging power of the United States, his writings and maps helped to shape a prevailing geopolitical culture of a country and empire entering into an uncertain era. One of the more disturbing aspects of much of his writings, especially from a vantage point of the early 21st century, is his frequent reference to race and 'English blood' as part of his explanation why certain racial groups were better able to govern and manage the world. He also, in his 1904 presentation to the Royal Geographical Society, identified the 'East' as perpetually threatening, unstable, and at times racially incapable of peaceful governance. Conjoining race and civilization, however, was not the sole preserve of Mackinder as American presidents such as Theodore Roosevelt often talked about the role of Americans in civilizing less fortunate others in Latin America and the Asia-Pacific region.

Woodrow Wilson's geographer: Isaiah Bowman and the 1919 Peace Conference

Shortly after entering the First World War, the United States President Woodrow Wilson created an Inquiry Committee. Colonel House and 150 members of the Committee produced 2,000 reports and 1,200 maps focusing on the ethnic, political, and historical boundaries of Europe. One of the key members was the geographer Isaiah Bowman, later President of Johns Hopkins University, who not only helped to create some of those maps but also contributed to a new geopolitical approach which sought to inform the American public about the First World War and the implications for Europe and the wider world. In 1915, Bowman was appointed director of the American Geographical Society (AGS) and he remained in post for the next 20 years. As a member of the Inquiry Committee, he ensured that the AGS was at the forefront of attempts to inform successive American administrations particularly about the post-First World War reconstruction of Europe.

Maps and Nazi Germany

After the 1919 Peace Conference, German geographers and cartographers began to produce new maps depicting a Germany imperilled and threatened by the new borders settled upon in Versailles. The maps, through their use of symbols, colour, and scale, drew attention to German-speaking communities outside the inter-war German state and to depict 'bleeding borders', which threatened German

economic interests as well by dividing up existing infrastructure. The German geographer Albrecht Penck also developed the notion of the German *Volks- und Kulturboden* that described German national identity in terms of cultural landscape. Under German influence, the countryside was well ordered and managed in contrast to that of its Slavic neighbours. As a consequence, a new Germany would not only retain all of the German Empire but also Austria and parts of Czechoslovakia. These maps depicting a 'Greater Germany' were widely reproduced in newspapers, magazines, posters, postcards, and school atlases. In terms of map production, the Weimar Republic was far more influential in shaping inter-war German cartographic culture.

By the early 1940s, when Nazi conquests had exceeded those lands and territories described as part of a 'Greater Germany', those earlier maps inspired by Penck were banned from Germany.

Bowman led the work of the Inquiry Committee for one year and later was critical in ensuring the liaison between mapmakers and their superiors at the Peace Conference. Professionally, he was appointed as Chief Territorial Specialist and the Committee was supposed to produce maps and charts which would help the American delegation to persuade European counterparts over particular territorial solutions for Eastern and Central Europe. Bowman was supported by regional specialists responsible for the Franco-German border, Poland and Russia, Austria-Hungary, the Balkans, and others areas such as the Far East. Those resulting maps were considered essential in the determination of the new geopolitical boundaries of Europe following the defeat of imperial Germany and the collapse of the Austro-Hungarian and Ottoman Empires.

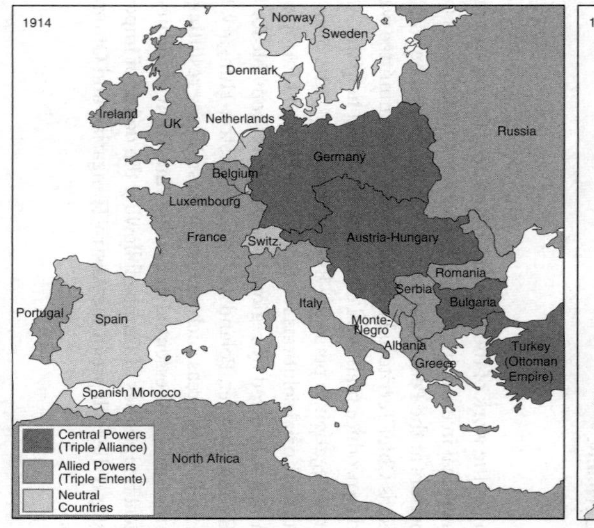

20. Europe in 1914 and 1919

Geographical intelligence was understood to be an important instrument of power. As Bowman explained to a colleague in England:

> Where the experts of [other] nations came fully stocked with ideas, they did not have the mass of information assembled in a flexible, workable form. Only the US delegation has such a resource, and we anticipated that this would give us a negotiating advantage even over the French, in whose capital city the fate of Europe and the Near East would be decided.

Bowman and the Inquiry Committee considered the production and shipment of maps and other data from New York to Paris to be both rational and strategic in ensuring that the principle of national self-determination within Europe could be informed by geographical data. Over 20 European peoples were identified as having the right to nationhood and the work of the Inquiry was instrumental in transferring territory and shifting national boundaries in the aftermath of the First World War.

When he arrived in Paris, Bowman discovered that the European delegations were deeply divided over the fate of port cities such as Danzig and the regional geographies of South-East Europe. In a manner reminiscent of later Euro-American squabbles over the conduct of the Global War on Terror, American negotiators were disappointed that their vision of a liberal internationalism existed uneasily with a Europe fixated on territorial boundaries and the ownership of specific places. But as Neil Smith, the author of the most definitive biography of Bowman has noted, this notion of a clash of geographical visions is flawed – American negotiators wanted the political boundaries of Europe settled so that they could then commence the really important business of creating open trading markets and networks. At the same time, of course, they ensured that America's territorial empire in Latin America and the Pacific was unchallenged by European colonial powers.

21. The Paris Peace Conference

Bowman published his textbook *The New World* (1921) and helped to create a new association called the Council on Foreign Relations. The Council's journal, *Foreign Affairs*, was to become a major outlet for foreign policy experts to consider the affairs of the United States in the wider world. Bowman believed, contrary to the isolationists, that America should play a central role in the development and evolution of the world economy. As his later work demonstrated, his vision (and accompanying maps) for the United States as a global power necessarily involved thinking through how power could be exercised at the expense of European colonial powers. For Bowman, power, if it were going to be exercised effectively over territories, would have to be informed by a commitment to free trade and diffused through international institutions in order to avoid the charge of American imperialism. He was later to be instrumental in providing specialist advice to the Franklin D. Roosevelt administration in the early 1940s, leading to the establishment of the United Nations. Its location in the American city of New York was testimony to how geographers such as Bowman were able to promote American national interests as simultaneously representing something more universal.

Why We Fight: Frank Capra and *The Nazi Strike* (1942)

The Italian-American film director Frank Capra was the driving force behind the creation of the award-winning *Why We Fight* series. Commissioned by the United States government, they were designed to show American servicemen and women why the country was engaged in war with enemies scattered around the world. Later it was shown to the American public as part of a propaganda drive to explain and legitimate involvement in the Second World War. The *Why We Fight* series contains seven one-hour films – *Prelude to War, The Nazi Strike, Divide and Rule, Battle of Britain, Battle of Russia* (Parts 1 and 2), *Battle of China,* and finally, *War Comes to America.* The latter was in some respects the most significant because it was intended to demonstrate why America could not remain isolationist with regard to global affairs.

In terms of the visual qualities of the series, *The Nazi Strike* is cartographically one of the most prominent. Hitler's plans for global domination are described and explained by direct reference to Mackinder's maps and famous geographical dictum:

> Who rules East Europe commands the Heartland
>
> Who rules the Heartland commands the World Island
>
> Who rules the World Island commands the World.

Viewers are informed that Hitler's strategic plans have been informed by the science of geopolitics and that, unlike other

22. The 'Heartland', from *The Nazi Strike* (1942)

nations, the German regime has collected and analysed information on places and their resources – both in terms of human and physical assets. As a consequence of their geopolitical perspectives, Hitler and his associates are depicted as hell-bent on securing ever more territory so that Germany can eventually claim the entire 'World Island' of Africa, Asia, and Europe. Given the demographic and physical resources of the World Island, the film suggests that it is only a matter of time before Germany controls the rest of the world including the Americas. The final image of that section of the film depicts the globe covered by a Nazi swastika.

The Capra series is just one, albeit important, example of how the geographical imaginations of American citizens were being stretched by the global conflict involving American troops in Europe, Africa, Asia, and the Pacific Ocean. Other filmmakers, journalists, and mapmakers such as John Huston, John Ford, and Charles Owens of the *Los Angeles Times* also played their part in revisiting the use of maps and their accompanying projections. Spurred on by Robert Strausz-Hupe's assertion that 'maps of every kind and description are the indispensable medium for diffusing the findings of geopolitics', these new maps were designed to show readers why Americans were fighting in particular places such as Guam. For West Coast audiences, the fighting in the Pacific was of particular interest, not least because so many servicemen were entering and leaving cities such as Los Angeles and San Diego in order to proceed to that war theatre – due west.

During the war itself, professional geographers were recruited to the American and British war effort. In Britain, for instance, geographers contributed to map production, photographic analysis, and the production of manuals and guides for military operations. Polar geographer Brian Roberts was commissioned to write guides on Iceland and the Arctic for British Naval Intelligence. There was no shortage of material for those academic contributors as by 1942 the Central Interpretation Unit had accumulated millions of photographs of continental Europe, taken by the Royal Air Force. These aerial photographs provided the basis for the construction of terrain models, which were considered to be essential in helping military planners interpret the places later to be targeted either for bombing and/or invasion.

These maps whether screened or drawn had lasting consequences on the collective Anglo-American geographical imaginations and provided a visual reservoir for later cartographers to explain and represent the cold war confrontation facing the United States and Western Europe after 1945. President Franklin D. Roosevelt was among the vanguard of this transformation and was given a huge globe as a Christmas present in December 1942. The advent of the cold war and the geopolitical confrontation with the Soviet Union transformed the strategic significance of Alaska and the high Arctic and new maps emphasizing the geographical proximity of the Soviet Union replaced those depicting the threat posed by Japan following its attack on Pearl Harbor in December 1941.

Cartography, geopolitics, and the cold war

Diplomatic historian Alan Henrikson has argued that the post-1945 period ushered into existence a shift in the collective geographical imagination from a continental to a nascent global outlook. Victory in 1945 did not bring public reassurance, however. If anything, events in the Pacific theatre of war alongside those in continental Europe confirmed that the United States could no longer take comfort in the fact that they were separated by thousands of miles from European and Asian centres of population. In the aftermath of that conflict, mapmakers and geographers such as Alexander De Seversky and Richard Edes Harrison deployed new polar-centred projections in order to emphasize the country's proximity to their cold war opponent, the Soviet Union. Harrison, who provided technical advice to the State Department and the Office of Strategic Services (later to become the CIA), was highly influential in promoting a view that Americans had to adapt to a rather different geographical state of mind from the one initiated when the country had entered into the First World War and participated in the 1919 Peace Conference.

Producing polar projections was just one element of this geographical revolution. Labelled air-age global geographers, Harrison in particular wanted to alert the American public to the geographical basics: the Earth is spherical and highly interconnected. Although the term globalization had yet to be invented, the articles and books in the United States in the immediate aftermath of the Second World War could be seen as an attempt to inculcate citizens with an understanding of those basic propositions. As a consequence of dominant cartographic projections such as Mercator, this new generation of post-war cartographers believed that too many Americans believed that the earth was flat rather than spherical. American strategic thinking needed to shift northwards and consider Dutch Harbor in Alaska rather than Pearl Harbor in Hawaii. The remedy for a new generation lay, so Harrison and his supporters believed, in adopting globes rather than maps because they were better able to represent relative distance and proximity.

The adoption of an aerial perspective also led to a new way of looking at the world, which not only emphasized the holistic qualities of the Earth but also encouraged a new way of thinking about distance in terms of flying hours. The polar perspective adopted by cartographers such as Harrison further cemented this sense of time-space compression. The lofty vantage of the North Pole helped to define the cold war zeitgeist. New projections such as the equidistant were judged to be most satisfactory because they depicted the world continuously and conveyed more accurately distance from one place to another. Polar-centred projections such as the ones popularized by Harrison were later to be adopted by military authorities and, with the help of a series of concentric circles, used to depict the operating range of bomber aircraft and missiles. The end result of the shift away from the Mercator projection was to persuade American personnel and their Soviet military counterparts to view the Arctic as the geopolitical barrier between the Americas and the Euro-Asian landmass.

General Arnold, the head of the US Army's air forces, wrote in *National Geographic* in 1946 that 'A surprise attack could readily come from across the roof of the world unless we were in possession of adequate airbases outflanking such a route of approach'. The development of the Distance Early Warning (DEW) line in the high Arctic was one of the most tangible expressions of this polar perspective, as the US military invested in a series of radar stations stretching from north-west Alaska to the eastern extremes of Canada in addition to Iceland and Greenland. From the mid-1950s onwards, the radar line, in conjunction with two others (Mid-Canada and Pinetree) was designed to detect incoming Soviet bombers and missiles. The DEW was the

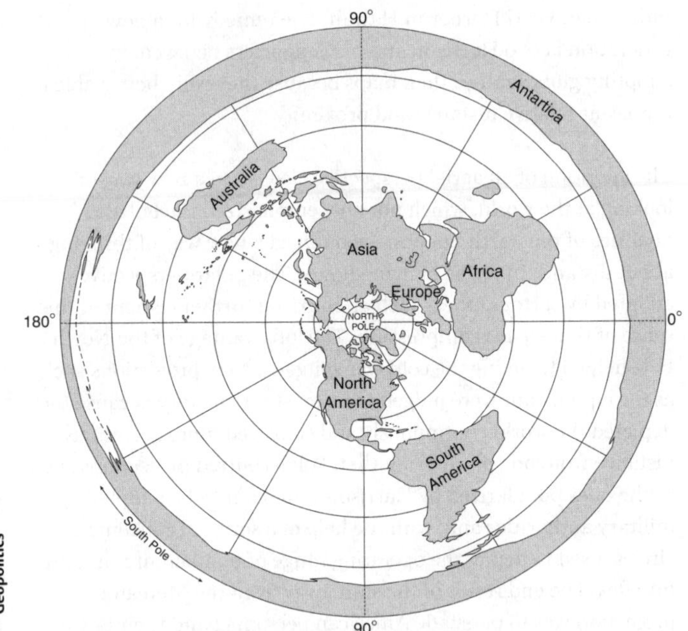

23. A polar-centred map projection

cornerstone of the North American Air Defense Command (NORAD). At its height, the DEW line involved 63 stations and stretched in effect for over 6,000 miles. For the Canadians, who operated the DEW stations in their northern territories, the creation of this cold war infrastructure helped to cement their sovereignty in the Arctic by giving them the means to survey their own territory.

> **Figure of the earth and the cold war**
>
> **During the cold war, cartographers and geodetic scholars highlighted the importance of developing a system for**

accurately locating places and their relative distances from one another. Any successful targeting of places by inter-continental ballistic missiles would depend upon this information. The term 'figure of the earth' is used to describe this process of determining the actual geographies of the Earth. With the growing tension between the two superpowers, American military establishments became ever more eager to obtain detailed information about the Eastern Bloc. New satellite systems such as CORONA, launched in 1958, were considered an essential element in the collection of geographical intelligence. During the Vietnam conflict, satellite photography was used to generate even more detailed maps of South-East Asia, which proved influential for American bombing missions, with dire consequences for civilians.

This heightened sense of geographical proximity was arguably one of the reasons why the United States and the Soviet Union and their respective governments were so wary of one another. By the time the Cuban missile crisis had erupted in the early 1960s, American and Soviet bombers were easily capable of traversing the Arctic Ocean and missile technology had moved on to the point whereby presidents and chairmen and their strategic advisors routinely talked about having merely minutes rather than hours to respond to a direct assault. This mental and geographical shrinkage also had implications for cold war popular culture as film, television programming, advertisements, and cartoons represented global shrinkage to their public audiences. Popular writers like Alastair Maclean penned thrillers such as *Ice Station Zebra* and *Night Without End*, which centred stories of intrigue and danger on the North Pole. Later converted into a Hollywood production, *Ice Station Zebra* in particular brought to the wide screen a visceral sense of how the Arctic was at the frontline of superpower confrontation.

American mapping of the Soviet threat

The cold war confrontation between the Soviet Union and the United States stimulated numerous representations of the menace posed by either side. In the case of American maps, the Soviet Union was often depicted as a Bear threatening neighbouring Europe. *Time,* in an article published in March 1952, depicted the Soviet Union as flowing blood-like towards Western Europe and in the process threatening to 'flood' or 'stain' the territories red. Other maps reproduced in *Saturday Evening Post* and *Life* depicted the Soviet Union as a gigantic octopus capable of interfering in the affairs of many states simultaneously.

After 40 years of cold war confrontation, the American geographical imagination had been well and truly shifted northwards. Successive generations came to appreciate that the United States and the Soviet Union were separated by an Arctic Ocean which no longer acted as any kind of physical barrier to inter-continental bombers and submarines capable of traversing under the icecap. By the end of the cold war in 1989–90, the DEW line had become an environmental hazard and political liability. American tourists were now travelling on former Soviet Union icebreakers to the North Pole, which was no longer inaccessible because of icecap melting. The geographical shift implied was significant, as the Arctic is now at the frontline of a rather different kind of engagement, in this case involving industrial pollutants and contamination from rusting cold war infrastructure.

The new Pentagon map: Thomas Barnett and post-9/11 United States

Thomas Barnett's 'The Pentagon's new map' was published in the magazine, *Esquire*, in March 2003. Composed in the aftermath of the 11 September attacks on the United States, Barnett's short article was accompanied by a map, which overturned cold war cartographies of East and West and even post-cold war cartographies of North and South. Described as a consultant to the Pentagon and faculty member of the US Naval War College, his new cartography of power and fear is based on a simple geographical division between gap and core. The significance of his mapping endeavours lies not only in terms of timing of publication but also because Barnett and other high-profile neo-conservative commentators such as Robert Kagan and Francis Fukuyama have become dominant in post-cold war and now post-9/11 America.

As at the end of the Second World War, the overturning of cold war cartographies led to a profound sense of geographical crisis in the 1990s. The mapping of the post-cold war period was carried out with some gusto as intellectuals and ideologues argued over the significance of the collapse of communist regimes including the fragmentation of the Soviet Union. For intellectuals associated with the Project of the New American Century, the Clinton administration's embrace of globalization and a multilateral world was considered dangerously misguided. Rather than entering into a world where cooperation and deterritorialized forms of governance would predominate, they believed that the United States had to be prepared to use its military and political hegemony to dominate a world that had arguably become more dangerous.

Maps, satellite photography, and intelligence: Saddam Hussein and the United States

The British journalist Robert Fisk recalled how a German arms dealer had told him of a meeting he had with officials in the Pentagon in the early 1980s:

'Mr Fisk . . . at the very beginning of the war, in September of 1980, I was invited to go to the Pentagon,' he said. 'There I was handed the very latest US satellite photographs of the Iranian front lines. You could see everything on the pictures. There were the Iranian gun emplacements in Abadan and behind Khorramshahr, the lines of trenches on the eastern side of the Karun River, the tank revetments – thousands of them – all the way up the Iranian side of the border towards Kurdistan. No army could want more than this. And I travelled with these maps from Washington by air to Frankfurt and from Frankfurt on Iraqi Airways straight to Baghdad. The Iraqis were very, very grateful!'

In terms of Barnett's mapping project, the world is unquestionably regarded as threatening, with terror networks and rogue states able to circumvent the geopolitical architecture of the global order. Being disconnected from the global community and its territorial mosaic of states is considered dangerous for those living in the core. In a world divided between a 'functioning core' and a 'non-integrating gap', Barnett's new map identifies those countries which share American values and those who do not. In effect, its simple bifurcation of the world contributes to a justification for projections of American power in particular territorial spaces such as Iraq and possibly Iran in the future.

Barnett claims that his vision was informed by a simple geographical epiphany – danger should be informed by a sense of where, not who. In other words, this geographical imagination, like Mackinder and other geopolitical authors before him, is concerned to identify and represent global dangers on a global scale. In his follow-up book, Barnett uses two maps to further extend his thesis of a world divided into two portions. In the first map, which was used in his *Esquire* article, the globe is divided into two portions and a blue stain radiates along the equator

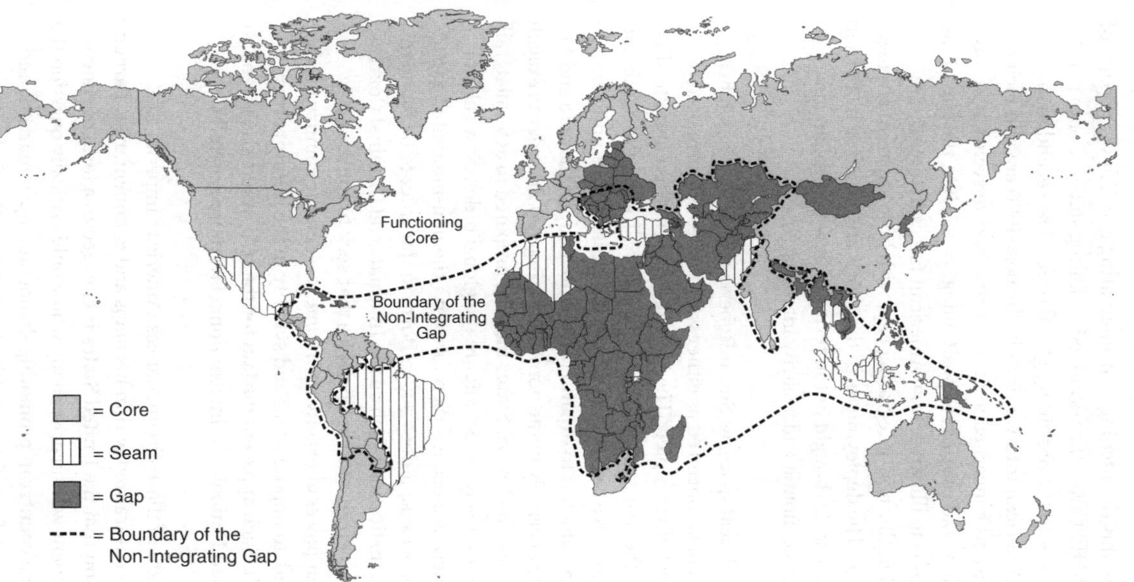

24. Barnett's functioning core and non-integrating gap

depicting this threatening non-integrating gap. These are parts of the world that are either occupied by failing states or ones poorly integrated into the prevailing global order. The second map depicts American interventions in the post-1990 era and includes all operations concerned with humanitarian intervention, combat, evacuation, and contingent positioning. In essence, the aim of the two maps is to illustrate how American forces frequently are involved in this non-integrating gap, with little apparent strategic advantage. The deployments in the 1990s are criticized by Barnett for being poorly thought out in terms of how they might aid America's economic and security interests.

Global political space, as Susan Roberts and other geographers have noted, is conceived as either well connected/formatted or disconnected/corrupted. The United States, in this computer-like world, is the manager and neo-liberal globalization the dominant programme. Barnett contends that the United States must pursue a strategy, which is to expand the membership of the core and to intervene decisively in the non-integrating gap. In order to execute these duties, the United States must be prepared to act unilaterally and pre-emptively to reconfigure the global order. New rules of engagement are needed therefore with the non-integrated gap, precisely because it does not conform to the order to be found in the core. Institutions such as the International Criminal Court (ICC) are perceived to be obstacles that seek to constrain American power at exactly the moment when the country needs a 'free hand' to impose order and stability in the unruly corners of the earth. Such apparent disdain for the ICC would also extend to the United Nations and international law more generally.

In the light of those circumstances, America's imperial role becomes naturalized within his maps and commentaries. Barnett's contention that the United States is engaged in a form of system management will surprise many who would critically question the role of the country in promoting democracy, open markets, and liberty in the face of its activities in the Third World during the cold war and its aftermath. Moreover, to assert that bin Laden and the Al-Qaeda network are 'pure products of the Gap' is a curious reading of an individual and group which owes its existence in part to cold war American foreign policy in conjunction with US–Saudi relations and US–Pakistani relations forged over the last 60 years. The Pentagon's new map is a dangerous fantasy and the experiences of post-2003 Iraq reveal how dangerous it can be for the US military to encourage democracy and open markets in a place where they are viewed by many as colonial occupiers and not a benign hegemony.

Conclusions

At the heart of geopolitics lies an interest in seeing the world and maps remain the favoured medium for depicting these so-called earthly realities. Critical geopolitical writers, along with historians of cartography, tend to be sceptical of anyone who claims that their maps are beyond political and geographical conceits and prejudices. Maps are conceived as instruments of power and states have long recognized the importance of mapping. Indeed it has been common for many countries, especially those with disputed boundaries and territories, to retain a tight control over the production and circulation of maps. In the case of Argentina and India, for instance, mapping is often carried out by their militaries. It also remains a federal offence in Argentina to produce maps which do not refer to the Falkland Islands as the Islas Malvinas and therefore an Argentine territory as opposed to a British one.

More generally, state-sanctioned maps can provide vital clues to a country's changing geopolitical imagination. While this chapter has concentrated on a few Anglo-American examples of changing mapping projections in the last hundred years, there is a longer and richer cartographic tradition spanning the Western, Islamic, and the Confucian worlds. In China, for example, new efforts are being made to raise the public's awareness of Africa as a social contact, as trading and economic investment between the two parties has increased. At the same time, however, other important moments in the historical geography of the People's Republic continue to be emphasized within school education and national media, such as the impact of the Japanese occupation of Manchuria in the 1920s and 1930s, the indivisibility of China and Taiwan, and the need to counter American hegemony in the Asia-Pacific region and beyond.

Chapter 6
Popular geopolitics

Have you watched recently films such as *Collateral Damage* (2001), *Behind Enemy Lines* (2001), *Tears of the Sun* (2003), and *United 93* (2005)? For many people, films are to be watched and enjoyed without necessarily reflecting on storylines, locations, or dialogue in any great detail. If you did reflect more deeply on their narrative content and visual form then you would be in the company of scholars contributing to a debate about 'film in an age of terror'. For the international relations scholar, Cynthia Weber, these films are important because they can be used to explore how the practical geopolitics of American foreign policy finds expression in the popular geopolitics of Hollywood. She explicitly focuses on what is called the 'moral grammars' of films. How are threats represented? Do parallels get drawn with September 11th? What kind of moral messages do we derive from films? If films play a part in informing and constructing personal and collective identities, what political and geographical understandings do we draw from shocking events such as September 11th?

Geopolitical representations and practices find expression, however, in a host of media including television, music, cartoons, the internet, and radio. For most people, these sources are highly important in terms of enabling access to information about current affairs or research on past events and people. Depending on geographical location and technological access, some if not all those media sources are available, especially in regions such as North America, Europe, and parts of Asia. Access to the internet in regions such as sub-Saharan Africa is patchy but the United States remains by far the most important generator in terms of materials placed on the web. The global dominance of the English language is significant in this regard. Age can also be a factor as well, as audience research has shown that for many young Americans, Jon Stewart's humorous *The Daily Show* is their most important source of 'news'.

In this chapter, I consider the role and potential impact of popular geopolitical representations of territory, resources, identity politics, and movement to be found in the media around the world. For the sake of brevity, some media forms such as films, television, radio, and the internet will receive more attention than others and in part this reflects my own personal predilections. Moreover, a great deal of the discussion is illustrated with reference to English-language media such as Hollywood, BBC World Service, and Voice of America rather than Arab-language newspapers, Iranian cinema, Chinese television, and Radio Moscow. Hopefully, this chapter will inspire the interested reader to explore media sources in other parts of the world.

Radio Farda and US–Iranian relations

Created in December 2002 and based in Prague, the State Department funded Radio Farda (meaning 'Tomorrow' in Farsi) as a form of public diplomacy. Broadcasting in Farsi, it aims to reach audiences in Iran and the Iranian diaspora and broadcasts music and news for listeners. The stated aim of the programming has been not only to promote a more positive vision of the United States but also to promote 'the struggle for freedom and self-determination in Iran'.

The Iranian government has reacted by purchasing jamming technology from Cuba in order to restrict the capacity of Iranian listeners to access Radio Farda. Moreover, Iran has also launched an Arabic-language television station, Al-Alam (The World), in an attempt to project Iranian influence in Iraq and beyond. This has been considered all the more significant as the Iranian government is accused by the United States of sponsoring terror organizations in Iraq and the Lebanon alongside developing its nuclear energy programme.

One of the most popular forms of electronic communication in Iran especially among the young is 'blogging', despite the Iranian government's practice of arresting bloggers for their online diaries, especially those that express political dissent.

Popular geopolitics and the media

It is perhaps surprising that geopolitical writers have not focused on popular geopolitics earlier, given the importance of the media in shaping our understandings and interaction with the world. Each of us has our own 'media signature', which is shaped by our access and interaction to various media including newspapers, radio, television, and the internet. These four media outlets are for most citizens in North America, Europe, and many parts of Asia and Oceania, readily available, often in a bewildering range of combinations, due to the large number of digital television channels available. Since the introduction of mass media in the 20th century, global connectivity has been intensified and accelerated. Media reporting in ways often perceived as undesirable conjoins people, places, and events.

The production, circulation, and consumption of news remains inherently uneven and unequal as some agents and communities are better able either to produce or access different sources. In terms of production, the Euro-American world leads under the control of large corporations such as CNN International, Time-Warner, News International, and the BBC. They are extremely significant in terms of determining broadcasting content and scheduling, notwithstanding national and international regimes, which can and do exercise some control over audience environments. The newspaper report, the television broadcast, and the internet podcast help determine which people, places, and events are judged to be newsworthy. Such choices then influence viewers' responses, with stories about victims and perpetrators, exploiters and exploited, named individuals and groups and the nameless. If pressed, for instance, most adults of a certain age can still recall where they were when they first heard the news and saw the images of President Kennedy's assassination in November 1963. For a later generation, the events surrounding the fall of the Berlin Wall in November 1989 and the 11 September 2001 attacks on the United States might easily generate a similar response.

Given the capacity of mass media if widely circulated to shape and influence public opinion both domestically and overseas, it is not surprising that governments have sought to regulate, monitor, disrupt, and ban broadcasting. The widespread publicity surrounding the release of photographs taken by US servicemen at the Abu Ghraib prison in Baghdad is a case in point. A documentary by the news channel CBS, broadcast to American viewers in April 2004, showed images taken on guards' digital cameras of Iraqi prisoners being degraded and tortured. The impact was immediate. The Bush administration was forced to make a rapid condemnation of the service personnel involved and insisted that it was the work of a 'few rotten apples'. For the critics of American foreign policy both inside and outside the United States, the photographs stood as a damning indictment of double standards when it came to the protection of human rights and liberal democratic norms. These images, already available on the internet, were circulated still further by those determined to violently resist the American occupation of Iraq.

Many viewers would then have used other media and social forums such as cafés and online message boards to discuss the meaning and significance of those photographs. Spectacular and shocking footage can and does make, for some viewers in the West at least, distant and remote places such as Iraq and more recently the Lebanon appear immediate and proximate. The caveat 'some' is significant as viewers' and listeners' emotional investments in places and events varies.

The geopolitical power of the media, therefore, lies not only in the broadcasting itself but also the manner in which events, people, and places are 'framed'. The latter is a term used in media studies to describe the way in which a story is explained to viewers or listeners. The recent events in the Lebanon and northern Israel are a case in point. For many viewers in Israel, the United States, and elsewhere, the Israeli bombing of the Lebanon was justified because of the military threat posed by Hezbollah operating out of southern Lebanon. The latter has been responsible for rocket attacks not only on northern Israel but also in the past for murderous assaults on Israeli military personnel and civilians in Israel and countries elsewhere such as Argentina. For others, the Israeli bombings and military invasion of southern Lebanon was disproportionate and calculated to inflict maximum damage on a civilian population. Either way, such images and news broadcasting brought to the fore two geopolitical imaginations which could not be reconciled.

Such images and news broadcasting can also act as provocation to governments, social movements, and others to demand action. Viewers might have reacted by phoning friends to commiserate, written letters to newspapers, emailed government departments, and composed podcasts. In different ways, therefore, the representations of places and people can and do provoke all kinds of emotional investments and demands for political action. In the case of the 2006 Israeli–Lebanese conflict, Western governments such as the United States, Britain, and France were forced to evacuate their own citizens from the region and pressurized into exploring modes of securing a ceasefire and the involvement of a United Nations peace-keeping force.

For many radicals in the Middle East and the Islamic world, the bombing of Lebanon will be subsumed into a larger visual and textual catalogue of Judaeo-Christian aggression against Muslim communities in a string of places including Afghanistan, Bosnia, Chechnya, Iraq, and Palestine. While images of dead children in Beirut have already been published in Western newspapers, far more shocking and graphic pictures are now widely available on the internet. Images can also have a long cultural afterlife. In October 2004, Osama bin Laden recalled via a broadcast posted on the internet how watching television pictures of tower blocks in Beirut being hit by Israeli jets provided him with the idea of assaulting American buildings. He was referring to the Israeli military action taken in June 1982. Two decades later his plan of action was implemented with deadly consequences.

Hollywood, the United States and national security cinema

For much of the last century, the United States has not experienced the ravages of war and mass disaster in a way that has been routine in some parts of the world. The assault on Pearl Harbor in December 1941 and the September 11th attacks are usually taken to be the two major exceptions to the rule. Despite the shock of both events and the loss of life, these two episodes pale into comparison with the losses experienced in places such as France, Belgium, and the Soviet Union. While many Americans died in Europe during the two world wars, such conflict did not penetrate American shores. American film companies, despite this absence of conflict on American territory, have been particularly significant in upholding the aphorism that war is often fought twice – once on the battlefield and once on film. As one of the characters in *Wag the Dog* (1997) tells his companions, 'war is show business'.

As America's direct experience of war is more limited, Hollywood generated a whole series of films, labelled 'national security cinema', which outlined in a highly imaginative way threats facing the United States. The list is a long one and includes Soviet and other communist forces, Nazis, terrorists, extraterrestrials, meteors, uncontrollable natural forces and machines. Given the widespread popularity of Hollywood productions both inside and outside the United States, it is understandable that films have been viewed as an important contributor to America's visions of its own standing and significance in the world. For many people outside the country, Hollywood films are usually their first point of contact with this country of 300 million inhabitants.

During the cold war, most Americans neither encountered a Soviet citizen nor travelled to the Soviet Union. The same could be said for Communist China and a host of other regimes of which the United States disapproved. The few that did were likely to be members of the armed forces, the business community, artists, sportsmen and women, and of course spies. For most Americans, Churchill's description of an 'iron curtain' across Europe seemed perfectly reasonable, as it did for many Europeans on either side of the Central/Eastern European divide. Film, radio, and later television footage played a crucial role in shaping American impressions of the Soviet Union and the threat posed by communism inside and outside their country. It also helped to consolidate in the main a sense of American self-identity – the land of the free, a beacon of democracy, and a liberal 'way of life' that President Truman had described in 1947.

Film historians have contended that American cold war cinema was at its most important in the 1940s and 1950s. In an era before mass ownership of television, people flocked to the cinema not only to watch films but also to access newsreels and documentaries shown alongside the main feature. What makes these films all the more significant is that Hollywood production companies were closely aligned to various organs of government departments such as the State and Defence Departments in Washington, DC. In 1948, the Pentagon established a special liaison office as part of the Assistant Secretary of Defense for Public Affairs and the latter was extremely important in shaping story lines and determining whether cooperation would be extended to any production wishing to use American military equipment or personnel. Films such as *The Longest Day* (1961) enjoyed Pentagon support even if some of the US military personnel had to be withdrawn from the filmset because of the worsening crisis in Berlin, which culminated with the East Germans building the wall which divided the city until November 1989.

The Pentagon had worked closely with producers such as Frank Capra and provided advice, equipment, and personnel for his *Why We Fight* series. The latter was required viewing for all US servicemen and women. This series in particular highlighted the significance attached to visual media by the American authorities in shaping military and public opinion. Given the scale of the threat apparently posed by the Soviet Union, it was not surprising that other agencies such as the US Information Agency and the Central Intelligence Agency (CIA) conceived of film as a vital element in the public campaign to educate American citizens about the dangers posed by the Soviets and to inform others outside the nation as well. The CIA provided secret funding for the animated film, *Animal Farm*, which was released in 1954, precisely because George Orwell's imprint was deemed to be highly appropriate given his allusions to the failed promises of the 1917 Russian Revolution.

During the 1940s and 1950s, Hollywood production companies did not need government funding or interference to persuade them that the Soviet Union and communism more generally posed a danger to the American way of life. America and the Soviet Union had, in this era, clashed over the future of Berlin and the Korean Peninsula. In 1949, the Soviets were confirmed as a nuclear power aided and abetted by the spy Klaus Fuchs. Films such as *My Son John* (1952), *Red Planet Mars* (1952), and *The Thing* (1951) made connections between the threats and dangers facing the American public in this uncertain period. While the first film highlighted the power of communism to influence and undermine the moral compasses of young people, the second and third focused on the dangers posed by aliens to the national security of the country. Taken together, the films seem to suggest that never-ending vigilance was required and that dangerous idealism regarding communism had to be contained.

As with the practical geopolitical reasoning of the Truman administration, films such as *My Son John* (1952) contribute to a particular geographical representation of the United States and its sense of self-identity. The openness and tolerance of the United States are shown to be both a virtue and a threat to its very existence. It is precisely because people, ideas, and goods can move freely throughout its national territory that loyal and patriotic citizens have to be ever vigilant. Given these kinds of conditions, impressionistic young people are portrayed as particularly vulnerable to such porosity and the malign influence of a certain type of intellectual. The Soviet Union, by way of contrast, was depicted as a Red Menace in a manner already outlined in the writings of George Kennan in documents such as NSC-68: geographically expansive, culturally monolithic, religiously suspect, and politically ceaseless in its desire to corrupt the body politic of America. According to some sections of Hollywood, this threat posed by the Soviets was also capable of subcontracting foreigners and possibly even space aliens to continue the struggle for world domination.

American political and religious figures such as William Buckley, Billy Graham, and John Foster Dulles also added to this potent discussion and dissection of the Soviet Union and the Red Menace. Graham in particular emphasized the profound differences between the godless Soviet Union and Christian America. Further cementing the popular significance of extremely conservative films like those described above was the political assault unleashed by the Committee on Un-American Activities of the House of Representatives (HUAC) in the late 1940s and early 1950s. The Committee opened its hearings in 1947 and heard submissions from 'friendly witnesses': producers, screenwriters, and actors associated with the motion picture industry. A total of 41 people were interviewed and a number of other people associated with the industry were accused of holding left-wing views.

Thereafter, the Committee concentrated its energies on the so-called 'Hollywood 10' – a group of individuals who refused to answer any questions and claimed the First Amendment of the US Constitution as their right to do so. The Committee disagreed with their stance and all were jailed for their dissent. With the help of the FBI, the Catholic League of Decency, and the American Legion, a list was produced called the *Red Channels*, which contained information about anyone working in Hollywood judged to have a subversive past. Unlike those who appeared before the Committee and convinced its members of their innocence, these individuals were blacklisted and effectively denied employment as writers, actors, or producers. Over 300 people including Charlie Chaplin and Orson Wells were listed as having suspect pasts. The impact on Hollywood was considerable and unsurprisingly did not encourage a visual culture of dissent from the predominantly conservative view of the cold war as a political-religious confrontation between the United States and its enemies.

This of course is not to presume that all producers, film critics, and movie watchers uncritically accepted the geopolitical representations of the Red Menace. Some producers used science fiction and the spectre of aliens to explore radically different interpretations of the cold war zeitgeist. Jack Arnold's *It Came from Outer Space* (1953) featured a group of visiting aliens condemning America's fear of strangers and the unknown. Small-town America is shown to be bigoted and xenophobic in its confrontation with strangers. Stanley Kramer's adaptation of *On the Beach* (1959) depicted the horrors of nuclear annihilation and questioned the strategic logic of nuclear confrontation. Despite government condemnation, the film was one of the highest grossing productions in the year of its release. Another film by Stanley Kramer, *High Noon* (1952), told the tale of a sheriff (Will Kane, played by Gary Cooper) who is refused help by local people even though a gang determined to extract revenge following their earlier arrest threatens his life. For some within Hollywood, the film was immediately seen as a satire on the activities of HUAC and the members of the motion picture industry who colluded with their blacklisting activities.

Between the late 1940s and 1960, the motion picture industry produced well over 4,000 films, with only a fraction genuinely critical of the conservative American understandings of the cold war and geopolitical representations of the Soviet Union and the communist threat. Hollywood, encouraged by the HUAC hearings and later the investigations conducted by Senator Joseph McCarthy, found it easier to produce films that reproduced rather than undermined those implicit understandings of the United States as a country composed of god-fearing, liberty-loving souls determined to resist being seduced by godless Soviets and their extraterrestrial accomplices.

In retrospect, it is clear that during the most intense phases of the cold war (the 1940s and 1950s) and later during the 1980s, Hollywood was at its most conservative in terms of its visual representations of the cold war. As a teenager, I vividly recall with some incredulity watching the film *Red Dawn* (1984), which opens with a parachute assault by Soviet and Cuban forces on an American school somewhere in the Mid West of America and eventually concludes with a group of schoolchildren successfully leading a counter-assault on these occupying forces. Other productions such as *Top Gun* (1986) seem to fit with a period characterized by renewed cold war tension, American determination to purge communist forces in Latin America and to financially and militarily assist others such as Afghan rebels in their resistance to the Soviet Union. While American service personnel or citizens inevitably prevailed, these kinds of films alongside *Firefox* (1984) and *Rambo Part II* (1986) either celebrated American technological prowess (and associated way of life) or depicted hypermasculine individuals able to overcome extreme odds. Fact and fiction frequently blurred as President Reagan made references to the filmic exploits of Rambo while explaining to the American people particular security threats facing the country.

The locations depicted in these late cold war films are significant as they often highlight the apparent danger posed by regimes found in Central America, South-East Asia, and the Middle East. One trend that was to become more apparent following the 1991 Gulf War was the emergence of films that depicted Islamic terrorists operating from places such as Beirut. This coincidence was not accidental as American forces had been disastrously deployed in the Lebanon in 1983. In October of that year, a truck bomb killed over 200 US Marines in their Beirut-based barracks. Shortly afterwards films appeared such as *Iron Eagle* (1985) and *Navy Seals* (1985), which took as their geographical backdrop either the Lebanon or the wider Middle East. Importantly, these places and their inhabitants were depicted as irrational, demonic, and prone to violence, especially against American and Western personnel and interests. In the case of *Top Gun*, which enjoyed substantial cooperation from the US Navy, the producers were told that the combat action had to be filmed over an ocean. During the film, the airborne location is described as somewhere over the

Indian Ocean and the enemy pilots are shown to have red stars embossed on their flight helmets but their identity is never confirmed. As the ocean closest to the Middle East, the possibility of those planes being from regional proxies of the Soviet Union is not implausible.

For Arab-American groups, these types of popular geopolitical representations were disturbing, precisely because they felt that a particular community was in danger of being aligned en masse with terrorism and anti-American activities. This fear was, of course, to be amplified after the American assault on Iraqi forces in Kuwait from January 1991 onwards. By that stage, it was apparent that the Soviet Union no longer posed a serious military threat to the United States, as the cold war confrontation was widely considered over, following the demolition of the Berlin Wall in November 1989. This did not imply, however, that it would not pose a threat to the United States ever again. When Hollywood did depict the post-cold war former Soviet Union in films such as *Goldeneye* (1995), *Air Force One* (1997), and the *Peacemaker* (1997), it was invariably represented as chaotic, fragmented, and a source of terrorism or arms trafficking. Alternatively, a production such as *Hunt for Red October* (1990), while raising the spectre of a possible naval assault on the United States, ultimately depicts a Soviet submarine captain and his fellow officers anxious to escape to the United States and enjoy the fruits of the American dream.

Before the September 11th attacks, post-cold war films concerning acts of terror in the United States were largely suggestive rather than grounded in substantial human experience. While there was an attack on the World Trade Center in 1993 and an attack on a Federal building in Oklahoma City in 1996, Hollywood did not respond in the same way as it did following 9/11. Films such as *Speed* (1994) and *The Rock* (1996) depicted acts of terror carried out by disgruntled American police and military officers angry with the federal government or specific institutions such as the

Los Angeles Police Department. Whereas the destruction of New York had been imagined cinematically in productions such as *Planet of the Apes* (1968), the deadly assault by 19 hijackers produced much existential discussion about the future of the United States, and Hollywood was quickly mobilized by the George W. Bush administration as one element in the response to this event and the subsequent self-declared War on Terror.

Films depicting terrorist attacks that were actually produced prior to 9/11 and then released in the aftermath were consumed in a rather different manner by American and international audiences. Productions such as *Collateral Damage* (2002) and *Sum of All Fears* (2001) were particularly significant in this regard and explored how Columbian and Russian extremists respectively successfully bomb American cities such as Baltimore, Los Angeles, and Washington, DC. In the case of *Sum of All Fears*, the plotline was changed so that Russian experts are shown to be converting a discovered Israeli nuclear device against a backdrop of American–Russian tension over Chechnya. In Tom Clancy's novel, the extremists are identified as Muslim and the Iranian President is later held to be directly responsible for the attack on the American Football stadium in Denver.

Behind Enemy Lines (2001) and US–European relations

Robert Kagan, the American strategic commentator, has noted how Americans and Europeans approach global politics rather differently. He claims that Europeans are more likely to seek refuge in multilateralism and international law as opposed to America's willingness to use military power and unilateral action. Hollywood films such as _Behind Enemy Lines_, which deals with the rescue attempts of the US Navy to save a downed airman in Serb-controlled Bosnia, have also reflected on this apparent division.

In a critical part of the film, the NATO commander (identifiably European) chastizes the American admiral leading the proposed rescue operation for his complete disregard for the mission's mandate. The American is asked to stand down his command. Later, however, the American admiral in a gesture of defiance to his NATO commanders leads a successful rescue mission and recovers the missing airman. Punished at the end of the film for his insubordination, the message of the film appears to be that sometimes America has to act unilaterally even if it makes it unpopular with others. Critically, the missing airman recovers aerial photography of mass graves in Serb-held Bosnia.

There is a great deal more that could be said on the films emerging in post 9/11 America, including those such as *United 93* (2005) which have begun the process of depicting and representing the attacks of September 2001. Four concluding points could be offered at this point. First, the motion picture industry in Hollywood has been and continues to be closely associated with organs of the American government, especially the Pentagon. Second, Hollywood films tend on the whole to be politically conservative and usually reflective of the prevailing political climate. Some films such as *Dr Strangelove* (1964) stand out in the history of American cold war cinema precisely because they appear to mock and ridicule the contemporary geopolitical situation and in this case the US–Soviet nuclear confrontation. In a rather different vein, Michael Moore's production *Fahrenheit 9/11* (2004) is noteworthy for its attempt to influence the 2004 presidential election. It failed to do so in the sense that President Bush was re-elected despite Moore's best efforts to depict his administration as suspect. Third, the representations of places and peoples in films matter. One only has to consider the concerns of Arab-Americans when films such as *The Siege* (1998) and *Rules of*

Engagement (2000) were released and depicted Arabs and Muslims as threatening to white and black Americans. Fourth, as Presidents Reagan and George W. Bush have shown, films can provide a visual tool to help citizens imagine and understand why America is planning a particular course of action. President Bush used the Iranian-made film *Kandahar* (2001) to justify American intervention in Afghanistan and the decision to engage militarily with the Taliban regime. In the film, an Afghan woman living in Canada is depicted trying to cross into Afghanistan in order to reach her suicidal sister. She never reaches her sibling and instead is forced to confront the poverty and deprivation endured by citizens of that country.

For a media-intensive culture such as the United States, films have considerable popular geopolitical significance. The vast majority of Americans are not well travelled and many post-9/11 films in particular have sought to provide comfort and reassurance in a period of insecurity and uncertainty. Latest post-9/11 productions such as *United 93* (2005) and *World Trade Center* (2005) seem to reinforce that trend as the latter film concentrates on individual acts of heroism amongst the buildings' ruins.

In the main they serve to reinforce particular geographical and moral understandings of the country (as an innocent victim of terror), just as earlier cold war films did against the backdrop of the Red Menace. As ever, the emotional investment and media signatures brought to bear by American and international audiences will inevitably vary.

News media and geographical framing: the case of Al-Jazeera

The concept of framing has been developed within media studies to explain how the mass media in particular draws public attention to certain topics involving people, events, and places. Framing thus highlights how journalists and media organizations

25. ***United 93*** **film poster**

organize and present news, which in turn may influence audience interpretations of those events and issues. As a form of agenda setting, selected frames such as 'the war on terror' or 'the war on drugs' imply particular interpretations, which favour certain understandings at the expense of others. Likewise place-based descriptions can be critically important in determining particular subject positions. This is particularly significant when a territory is contested and labelled in different manners by opposing communities. Imagine the public outrage if an Argentine television broadcast ever referred to the Islas Malvinas as the Falkland Islands. This might be taken to be deeply unpatriotic, given that successive Argentine governments have protested that the islands were illegally annexed by Britain in 1833. Likewise, similar outrage might be provoked if a Palestinian news broadcaster ever referred to Judea and Samaria rather than the West Bank or the Occupied Territories. While both cases are highly unlikely, it is perhaps not surprising that both Argentines and Palestinians would be highly sensitive to how other broadcasters described these disputed territories, especially organizations originating from countries such as the United States.

Television broadcasters are an important source of framing and in particular those with a reputation for international coverage or large audiences such as CNN or the BBC. Another organization is the Qatari-based Al-Jazeera news channel, which was launched in 1996. Supported by the Emir of Qatar, the station operates from a small Persian Gulf country, which just happens to contain some of the largest natural gas reserves in the world alongside a large American airbase used to launch the invasion of Iraq in 2003. Unlike other Arab-language news organizations, Al-Jazeera quickly established a reputation for a rather different style of news broadcasting and opinion-forming programming, albeit operating out of a country where the Ministry of Information was abolished in 1998, thus ending government censorship of the press, radio, and television. Within the Middle East, the latter is by far the most significant media outlet because newspaper readership is comparatively low by Western standards.

Seemingly unperturbed by criticism from regional governments such as Saudi Arabia and Egypt, it has introduced path-breaking discussion programmes such as *The Opposite Direction*, *Only for Women*, and *More than One Opinion*, which have been willing to tackle controversial social, cultural, and political issues such as women's rights and Islamic extremism. Its television presenters and journalists such as Dr Faisal al-Qasim have become household

26. A still from Al Jazeera TV, taken on 7 September 2006

names not only in the Middle East but also amongst the Arabic-speaking diaspora in North America, Europe, and elsewhere. It was also the first Arabic-language news channel to broadcast Israeli officials and government ministers speaking in Hebrew.

Al-Jazeera's broadcasting reputation within the Middle East was largely cemented by its coverage of the US–UK bombing campaign of Iraq in December 1998. Codenamed Operation Desert Fox (the given name of the German General Rommel during the Second World War), the Qatari-based news organization showed television footage of the impact of 70 hours of continuous missile attacks on Baghdad and elsewhere in the country. Its footage was rapidly sold to other television stations around the world. Later, the Saddam Hussein regime, recognizing the widespread appeal of Al-Jazeera amongst Arabic-speaking audiences, sent officials such as the English-speaking Deputy Prime Minister Tariq Aziz to explain to viewers in Arabic and English the impact of the attack. While the television station was widely condemned both in the region and elsewhere for being a propaganda mouthpiece of Saddam Hussein's regime, the footage was arguably contributing to a rather different geographical framing of Iraq. Even if British and especially American media were content to condemn the regime for unquestionable acts of brutality, this kind of footage contributed to a view of Iraq as an inhabited and civilized place in which ordinary people were bearing the brunt of UN-imposed sanctions and now further acts of bombing by Western powers.

At the same time, Al-Jazeera's broadcasting reputation was further enhanced (or possibly diminished depending on your political point of view) when it became the media organ of choice for Osama bin Laden and his associates. Broadcast in December 1998, an interview lasting 90 minutes with bin Laden was followed up by further appearances on the television channel in 1999. These in combination with Al-Jazeera's interviews with Iraqi ministers were criticized by regional governments such as Saudi Arabia and Kuwait because they felt that it gave further publicity to terrorists and tyrants. However, the visual impact of these broadcasting programmes also challenged some of the existing geographical and political representations of these individuals and regimes as demonic, irrational, or simply mad. In particular, bin Laden's location somewhere in Afghanistan in a cave was notable in highlighting his austere existence in sharp contrast to the regimes in Egypt, Saudi Arabia, and Pakistan, which he condemned as corrupt, decadent, and un-Islamic.

As with its subsequent coverage of the Palestinian Intifada in 2001, Al-Jazeera's televisual footage of the uprising on the West Bank and the military response by the Israeli security forces was instrumental in raising the international profile of the region and its inhabitants. The footage not only placed Arab governments under pressure but also caused the Israelis and Americans to rethink their media and political strategies for the Middle East. The Israeli Broadcasting Authority began to develop an Arabic-language television channel. During the Intifada itself, the

Palestinian Authority temporarily closed the Al-Jazeera bureau office at Ramallah in protest at a programme subsequently broadcast about the PLO in the aftermath of the Israeli invasion of the Lebanon in 1982. Therefore, Al-Jazeera has continued to cajole, provoke, and pressurize governments within the Middle East and beyond.

As a consequence of its footage in Afghanistan and Iraq, it has earned the opprobrium of the American and British governments for its willingness to broadcast graphic images of victims killed by Allied bombs and missiles as well as claims by the Taliban and resistance forces in both those countries about Allied losses. Infamously, their Kabul-based bureau was bombed by an American missile, killing a reporter, following complaints from the Bush administration for their reporting which incidentally is independent of any press pool arrangements. This assault occurred at a time when the US government was in the midst of a public diplomatic campaign following 9/11 to convince Muslims around the world that Muslims living in the United States were accepted and welcomed by the wider community. The 'Shared Values' campaign, launched by Under-Secretary of State for Public Diplomacy, Charlotte Beers, appeared by 2002 to a have little impact on Arab public opinion in particular.

The most important legacy with regards to geographical framing is the manner in which Osama bin Laden has continued to use Al-Jazeera as a favoured medium for broadcasting his messages to the wider world. With the speed of modern telecommunication networks, his Afghan base has not proved to be a geographical disadvantage in allowing him to use the media to deliver messages. These broadcasts are held responsible for inflaming anti-American and anti-Israeli sentiment in the region. In an interview conducted in October 2001 with Al-Jazeera's Kabul-based reporter, Taysir Alluni, bin Laden used this opportunity to repeat his assertion that the 11 September attacks on the United States were as an act of defence in the light of

American double standards over the Israeli occupation of Palestine and its neo-colonial assault on Iraq and Afghanistan. While widely condemned and deplored by many governments and communities for his support of terrorism and anti-Semitism, his explanation with its propensity to geographically link grievances such as Palestine, Iraq, and Bosnia finds a sympathetic audience, especially in those countries such as Egypt and Pakistan which have historically been closely tied to the United States.

Frustratingly for the Bush administration, the offer of a $5 million bounty for his capture has not been realized and bin Laden continues to challenge the geographical framing of the US as a 'crusading state'. His own particular form of popular geopolitics blends geographical cross-referencing, historical analogies, critiques of colonialism, and classical scriptures and traditions of Islam to apparent great advantage. Aided and abetted by some of the reporting footage provided by Al-Jazeera (albeit unwittingly on their part) in Afghanistan, Iraq, and Palestine alongside other visual media such as suicide videos and postings on the internet, bin Laden is able to construct a very different kind of vision of the Middle East and the wider Islamic community as one that is imperilled and threatened by Western interventions. His use of the term 'crusading' is also significant because it conjures up only too easily images of past episodes of Christian soldiers assaulting the Muslim peoples of South West Asia. Making specific and selective historical and geographical connections remains a critical element in his messages.

The internet and a popular geopolitics of dissent

Since the 1980s, the growth and development of the internet has been widely championed as encouraging further social interaction and shrinking geographical distance. The United States remains by far the biggest user community of the internet and the most significant producer of information. The digital divide between North America, Europe, and East Asia, on the one hand, and sub-Saharan Africa and the Middle East, on the other, remains stark, even though internet access is becoming more widespread in both the latter regions. Powerful search engines such as Google allow users to access and download images and stories in mere seconds with both positive and negative consequences, ranging from the fear of seditious and offensive material being published on the internet to people being able to access new communities and social networks in a virtual manner. This has clearly allowed all kinds of activities to flourish, including global terror networks and neo-Nazi groupings. Al-Qaeda has used the internet to generate funding, send encoded messages to members, publicize videos of speeches by its leaders, and to promote activities across the world. Much to the frustration of national governments, the internet is extremely difficult to police and patrol as websites can be shut down but then re-emerge shortly afterwards with a different domain address.

The internet has provided an important medium for the anti-globalization movement and enabled it to challenge both the material power of states, corporations, and institutions associated with the dominant political-economic order and to contest particular visual and textual representations of that dominant architecture. In the case of the first dimension, the anti-globalization movement has publicized and organized global days of action, usually in cities which happen to be hosting meetings of the WTO, IMF, or the G8. More widely, the internet has facilitated the growth and development of social networks such as the People's Global Action and the World Social Forum, both of which have enabled activists all over the world to come together to consider alternatives to neo-liberalism and solutions to local issues such as water privatization in South Africa, land ownership in Mexico, and the impact of foreign debt repayments in Latin America.

The internet has therefore allowed individuals and groups committed to protesting about neo-liberal forms of globalization

27. Labour unions and supporters rallying at the 1999 WTO meeting in Seattle. Mostly peaceful demonstrations led to a police crackdown

to exchange experiences, plan action, swap dates, and highlight future events in a way that it clearly far quicker than in the past. The demonstrations organized during a World Trade Organization (WTO) meeting in Seattle during November and December 1999 coincided with what has been called e-mobilization and e-protest. Moreover, the capacity to circulate images alongside commentaries has also been important in allowing these groups to promote their particular viewpoints and potentially to shape the news agendas, even though many campaigners complain that mainstream media tends to marginalize their protests and demands for radical reforms of the neo-liberal world economy and its servicing institutions such as the WTO or powerful groupings such as the G8.

Contesting dominant representations of the prevailing global politico-economic order is another area of activity facilitated by the internet and other media. Corporate television broadcasts of G8 and WTO summits tend, in the opinion of anti-globalization movements, to reinforce rather than challenge the geopolitics of neo-liberalism. Attention is usually granted to heads of states and their delegations as opposed to protestors who tend to be viewed as a distraction or, increasingly in the aftermath of 9/11, as a security challenge which needs to be contained. As the ownership of the media becomes increasingly concentrated in the hands of larger corporations such as News International, this tendency is likely to increase rather than diminish. As with powerful economies such as the United States and Japan, there is a tendency to support the politico-economic status quo and that includes its accompanying political architecture, which helps to regulate the interaction between territories and flows of people, investment, and trade.

Websites and alternative media sources (e.g. www.indymedia.org.uk) have been used routinely to convey a rather different vision of the world – an unequal one where the richest 20 per cent of the world possess 90 per cent of global income. These sites have also encouraged campaigners to submit news stories and images of global days of action and to submit items about local places and their geographical connections to global processes such as trade, investment, and foreign debt. The Zapatista movement in Mexico and its leadership have pioneered much of this investment in the internet and alternative media, recognizing in the early 1990s that the media were a crucial component in their struggles to resist the Mexican state, international financial markets, and the prevailing global economic order. What made their usage so surprising was that internet connectivity was low in Southern Mexico. Within two years of launching their counter-offensive against neo-liberalism, the Zapatistas had organized a series of continental and intercontinental meetings in 1996 and 1997 through the use of the internet and email. Thousands attended the meetings and exchanged information with one another, including the American film producer Oliver Stone. The charismatic leader of the Zapatistas (Marcos) used the internet to publicize their causes (land dispossession, economic marginalization, and racial discrimination) and encouraged new networks of solidarity in Mexico, Latin America, and beyond. The internet provides a forum for the group to continue their struggle and is also successful in encouraging other groups and individuals to formulate alternative understandings of the global economy, international financial markets, and the Mexican economy.

As other governments have discovered, controlling information posted on the internet can be controversial and difficult, given the efforts of hackers to undermine government established firewalls. In the aftermath of 9/11, the US Congress passed the Patriot Act, which enables the Executive and key agencies such as the National Security Agency to investigate internet and email traffic of those suspected of engaging in activities likely to be harmful to the United States. Other states such as Britain have also sought to impose greater surveillance and control over information users considered suspect. The monitoring of individuals and groups, in the name of counter-terrorism, has been extremely significant in terms of governments trying to restore the prevailing geopolitical architecture of sovereign states, borders, and national territories. In the case of China, the government simply insisted that the Chinese version of Google prevented users from accessing banned pro-democracy websites and images relating to the Tiananmen Square massacre. The internet search engine provider agreed to those restrictions because it was eager to maintain a good 'search experience'. A number of hackers, many of whom are based in the United States such as the *Cult of the Dead Cow* (www.cultdeadcow.com) remain determined to crack the firewalls established by the Chinese government designed to restrict access to banned websites.

Conclusions

This chapter has shown how popular geopolitics can be studied with reference to the media and clearly could be extended to consider in greater detail others such as radio or music. While established media forms such as newspapers, television, and radio remain highly significant in producing and circulating news about the world, it is new media forms such as the internet and associated practices such as blogging and podcasting that will command increasing attention from those interested in popular geopolitics. As interconnectivity increases, especially in the Middle East, the internet is providing not only an opportunity for viewers to access different news sources but also to articulate their opinions online. In countries and regions where the public sphere is tightly controlled by national governments, bloggers are an increasingly significant presence even if their activities have been subject to harassment, imprisonment, and ongoing surveillance. Iranian bloggers provide fascinating insights into contemporary Iran and offer dissenting opinions with regards to Iran's foreign policy choices, which help explain to interested readers why, for example, many online commentators feel threatened by the military powers of the United States, Israel, Pakistan, India, and China. Unlike Iran, all these states possess substantial stocks of weapons of mass destruction.

We should not, for one moment, assume that new media practices such as blogging are not important in other places too. In the United States, liberal academics and commentators have frequently bemoaned the fact that so much of American mainstream media is corporately owned and supportive of the Bush administration's Global War on Terror. Frustrated at the lack of opportunity to express dissenting views, websites such as Think Progress (www.thinkprogress.org) and Daily Kos (www.dailykos.com) monitor mainstream media and right-wing blogs and highlight distortions with regard to contemporary American domestic and foreign policy debates. One of the most significant interventions by Think Progress was to demand that ABC television make changes to their documentary screened in September 2006 on *The Path to 9/11*. Critics contended that the documentary was seriously mistaken and libellous in its depiction of the Clinton administration as tardy and unresponsive to the growing threat posed by Islamic militants. ABC was forced to remove passages of the programme which suggested that the Monica Lewinsky affair distracted President Clinton from pursuing national security matters. With the support of former Clinton administration officials, these internet sites are providing an important counterblast not only to mainstream justifications for the continued War on Terror but also to the belief amongst Bush supporters that only the Republicans can secure America from the threat posed by Islamic militancy. In these uncertain times, it remains essential to think geopolitically.

References

Chapter 1

Churchill's speech is at: http://www.churchillspeeches.com/
Truman's speech is available at:
http://www.presidency.ucsb.edu/ws/index.php?pid=12846
G. W. Bush's State of the Union addresses for 2002 and 2003 are available at: http://www.whitehouse.gov/news/releases/2002/01/20020129-11.html and http://www.whitehouse.gov/news/releases/2003/01/20030128-19.html respectively.
President Ahmadinejad is reported at:
http://www.guardian.co.uk/iran/story/0,12858,1601413,00.html
Savage's comments can be found at:
http://www.commondreams.org/views03/0620-02.htm
Bill Clinton's 1999 speech is available at:
http://www.pbs.org/newshour/bb/europe/jan-june99/address_3-24.html

Chapter 2

Gearóid Ó Tuathail, *The Geopolitics Reader* (Routledge, 2006), p. 1.
Frederick Sondern, 'The Thousand Scientists behind Hitler' *Readers Digest*, 1941).
Edmund Walsh, *Total Power* (Doubleday, 1948), p. 21
H. Kissinger, *The White House Years* (1979), p. 598, and his comments about Chile are available at:
http://en.wikipedia.org/wiki/Chilean_coup_of_1973

Chapter 3

J. Nye, 'The Decline of America's "Soft Power"', *Foreign Affairs,* 83 (2004), 20.

Chapter 4

W. H. Auden's poem: http://www.gametec.com/poemdujour/Sept1.1939.html

P. van Ham, 'The Rise of the Brand State', *Foreign Affairs,* 80 (2001), 2.

W. Connelly, *Identity/Difference* (University of Minnesota Press, 2002), p. 64.

J. Agnew, *Making Political Geography* (Arnold, 2002), p. 143.

Chapter 5

F. D. Roosevelt's radio address is available at: http://www.presidency.ucsb.edu/mediaplay.php?id=16224&admin=32

Yves Lacoste, 'An Illustration of Geographical Warfare', *Antipode,* 5 (1973), 1.

H. Mackinder, 'On Thinking', in M. Sadler (ed.), *Lectures on Empire* (printed privately, 1907), p. 37, and 'The Geographical Pivot of History', *Geographical Journal,* 13 (1904), p. 422. His 'dictum' referred to in *The Nazi Strike* comes from *Democratic Ideals and Reality: A Study in the Politics of Reconstruction* (Constable & Co., 1919), p. 60

Bowman: American Geographical Society Archives, Bowman Papers: Letter from Bowman to Frank Debenham, July 12, 1929.

R. Strausz-Hupe, *Geopolitics: The Struggle for Space and Power* (G. P. Putnam & Sons, 1942), p. 7.

Robert Fisk: http://www.countercurrents.org/fisk070107.htm

Further reading

Much of the information relating to geopolitical matters available on the web is subject to great change and variation in quality. Online magazines such as *Monthly Review* (www.monthlyreview.org) and journals such as *Geopolitics* and *Political Geography* regularly publish geopolitical analyses. For French-speaking readers, the journal *Herodote* is an excellent starting point and for Italian-speaking readers, the Italian Journal of Geopolitics, *Limes,* would be of interest. More generally, search engines such as Google (www.google.com) provide ample opportunities to explore the term geopolitics further.

Chapter 1

J. Agnew, *Geopolitics* (Routledge, 2003)
K. Dodds, *Global Geopolitics: A Critical Introduction* (Pearson Education, 2005)
C. Flint, *Introduction to Geopolitics* (Routledge, 2006)
C. Flint and P. Taylor, *Political Geography* (Pearson Education, 2006)
G. Ó Tuathail, *Critical Geopolitics* (Routledge, 1996)
G. Ó Tuathail, S. Dalby, and P. Routledge (eds), *The Geopolitics Reader* (Routledge, 2006)

Chapter 2

B. Blouet, *Halford Mackinder* (University of Texas Press, 1987)
I. Bowman, *The New World* (World Company, 1921)
K. Dodds and D Atkinson (eds), *Geopolitical Traditions* (Routledge, 2000)

T. Garton Ash, *Free World* (Random House, 2004)
D. Haraway, *Primate Visions* (Routledge, 1989)
M. Heffernan, *The Meaning of Europe* (Arnold, 1998)
O'Hara, S. L., and Heffernan, M., 'From Geo-strategy to Geo-economics: The "Heartland" and British Imperialism before and after Mackinder', *Geopolitics*, 11/1 (2006), 54–73.
G. Parker, *Geopolitics: Past, Present and Future* (Pinter, 1998)
W. Parker, *Mackinder: Geography as an Aid to Statecraft* (Oxford University Press, 1982)

Chapter 3

J. Agnew, *Hegemony: The New Shape of Global Power* (Temple University Press, 2005)
J. Agnew and S. Corbridge, *Mastering Space* (Routledge, 1995)
M. Begg, *Enemy Combatant* (Free Press, 2006)
P. Dicken, *Global Shift* (Sage, 2003)
F. Fukuyama, *After the Neocons* (Profile Books, 2006)
G. Gong (1984) *The 'Standard of Civilization' in International Society* (Oxford University Press, 1984)
M. Hardt and A. Negri, *Empire* (Harvard University Press, 2001)
D. Harvey, *The New Imperialism* (Oxford University Press, 2005)
S. Krasner, *Sovereignty: Organised Hypocrisy* (Princeton University Press 1999)
S. Nye, *Soft Power* (Public Affairs, 2004)
P. Sands, *Lawless World* (Penguin, 2005)
N. Smith, *American Empire* (University of California Press, 2003)
M. Steger, *Globalization: A Very Short Introduction* (Oxford University Press, 2003)

Chapter 4

L. Bialasiewicz, 'The Uncertain State(s) of Europe', *European Urban and Regional Studies* (2007, forthcoming)
M. Billig, *Banal Nationalism* (Sage, 1995)
G. Dijkink, *National Identity and Geopolitical Visions* (Routledge, 1996)
D. Gregory, *The Colonial Present* (Blackwell, 2004)
S. Huntington, 'The Clash of Civilisations', *Foreign Affairs*, 72 (1993), 22–49.

B. Lewis, *The Crisis of Islam* (Phoenix, 2004).
E. Said, 'The Clash of Ignorance', *The Nation* (22 Oct 2001), available at: www.thenation.com
A. Smith, *National Identity* (Penguin, 1991)
A. Smith, *Chosen Peoples* (Oxford University Press, 2003)

Chapter 5

D. Gregory and A. Pred (eds), *Violent Geographies* (Routledge, 2006)
M. Heffernan, *The Meaning of Europe* (Arnold, 1998)
G. H. Herb, *Under the Map of Germany* (Routledge, 1997)
C. Jacob, *The Sovereign Map* (University of Chicago Press, 2006)
M. Monmonier, *How to Lie with Maps* (University of Chicago Press, 1996).
J. A. Pickles, *A History of Spaces: Cartographic Reason, Mapping and the Geo-Coded World* (Routledge, 2004)
S. Roberts, A. Secor and M. Sparke, 'Neoliberal Geopolitics', *Antipode*, 35 (2003), 886–97
S. Schulten, *The Geographical Imagination in America* (University of Chicago Press, 2001)
D. Wood, *The Power of Maps* (Guildford Press, 1992)

Chapter 6

M. Power and A. Crampton (eds), *Cinema and Popular Geopolitics* (Routledge, 2006)
J. Sharp, *Condensing the Cold War* (University of Minnesota Press, 2000)
R. Toplin, *Michael Moore's Fahrenheit 9/11* (University of Kansas Press, 2006)
J.-M. Valantin, *Hollywood, the Pentagon and Washington* (Anthem Press, 2005)
C. Weber, *Imagining America at War* (Routledge, 2005)

Index

A

B

C

D

E

F

G

H

I

J

K

L

M

V

W

Y

CAPITALISM

A Very Short Introduction

James Fulcher

The word 'capitalism' is one that is heard and used frequently, but what is capitalism really all about, and what does it mean? Fulcher addresses important present day issues, such as New Labour's relationship with capitalism, the significance of global capitalism, and distinctive national models of capitalism. He also explores whether capital has escaped the nation-state by going global, emphasizing that globalizing processes are not new. He discusses the crisis tendencies of capitalism, such as the Southeast Asian banking crisis, the collapse of the Russian economy, and the 1997–1998 global financial crisis, and asks whether capitalism is doomed. The book ends by asking whether there is an alternative to capitalism, discussing socialism, communal and cooperative experiments, and the alternatives proposed by environmentalists.

http://www.oup.co.uk/isbn/0–19–280218–6

GLOBAL WARMING

A Very Short Introduction

Mark Maslin

Global Warming is one of the most controversial scientific issues of the twenty-first century. This is a problem that has serious economic, sociological, geopolitical, political, and personal implications.

This *Very Short Introduction* is an informative, up-to-date, and readable book about the predicted impacts of global warming and the surprises that could be in store for us in the near future. It unpacks the controversies that surround global warming, drawing on material from the recent report of the Intergovernmental Panel on Climate Change (IPCC), and for the first time presents the findings of the Panel for a general readership. The book also discusses what we can do now to adapt to climate change and mitigate its worst effects.

http://www.oup.co.uk/isbn/0–19–284097–5